Stencilling

TECHNIQUES FOR INTERIORS, FURNITURE & OBJECTS

JILL VISSER & MICHAEL FLINN

LITTLE, BROWN

For Bob and Donna

With thanks for painting, fixing, making, hanging and for constant support

A LITTLE, BROWN BOOK

Text © Jill Visser
Illustrations © Little, Brown and Company (UK)

First Published in Great Britain in 1989 by Macdonald & Co (Publishers) Ltd

This Paperback edition published by Little, Brown in 1993

Reprinted 1994, 1995

British Library Cataloguing in Publication Data
Visser, Jill
Stencilling.
1. Stencil work
I. Title   II. Finn, Michael
745.7'3   NK8654
ISBN 0-316-90695-6

Colour separation by British Art, Hong Kong
Filmset by Bookworm Typesetting Ltd

Printed in Italy by Graphicom

Senior Editor: Judith More
Editor: John Wainwright
Art Director: Bobbie Colgate-Stone
Designer: Miranda Kennedy
Photography: Jerry Tubby
Stylist: Jill Visser
Indexer: Margaret Cooter
Illustrator: Val Hill

Little, Brown and Company (UK)
Brettenham House
Lancaster Place
London WC2E 7EN

PICTURE CREDITS
All photographs by Jerry Tubby except for:
Aldus Archive: 11; American Museum in Britain: 6, 9, 10; Campbell Smith & Co, London: 14; Hunterian Art Gallery: 15; Pavillion, Edinburgh: 45, 54, 76, photos by John Brown; Pipe Dreams: 73b; Jessica Strang: 58, artist Lyn Le Grice; Victoria & Albert Museum: 7, 12; Elizabeth Whiting & Associates: 24, 31, 42, 48t, 55, 57, 75, 94, artist Lyn Le Grice.

CONTENTS

THE HISTORY OF STENCILLING

NINETEENTH CENTURY ROOM

This New England bedroom with its stencilled wall, bedspread and chair (at the American Museum, Claverton Manor, Bath), is a reconstruction based on an original from the early nineteenth century.

The early development of stencilling is not easy to trace, as the first stencils were cut from perishable materials, and few have survived. But it is likely that many different civilisations around the world were practising their own techniques around the same time.

Whilst the word stencil originates from *estencler*, French for 'to sparkle', and the Latin *scintilla*, meaning a spark, and although there is evidence that stencilling was used by prehistoric man, it is accepted generally that it was the Chinese who originated the process, before 3000 BC. It is also known that stencils made of dried sealskin were used by the early Eskimos of Baffin Island, and that around 2500 BC the Egyptians were stencilling mummy cases.

China

The Chinese are thought to have originated the process of stencilling before 3000 BC. Evidence includes the famous discoveries by Sir Aurel Stein, a British Orientalist, of items dating from 500–1000 AD which were decorated with patterns resembling a stencilled form. The discovery, at the Caves of The Thousand Buddhas, Tunhuang, West China, included silks displaying stencilled Buddha figures, as well as some tough paper on which various designs were outlined with a mass of minute pinpricks. The outlines were transferred onto the paper by pounding powdered charcoal though the holes, and were then filled in by hand.

The Chinese also invented a special stencil technique called 'Derma Printing', which involved using an acid ink which ate into the paper as the pattern was being drawn.

Fiji

Natives of the Fiji Islands traditionally used stencilled designs on clothing, and anthropologists have theorised that the shapes were adopted from holes bored into banana and bamboo leaves by the larvae of local insects. The Fijians used a selection of colours derived from vegetable dyes, charcoal and water, and red earth liquified with sap from the candlenut tree.

Japan

With the opening of trade routes from China, the use of stencils spread to other oriental and middle eastern countries. In Japan, stencilling dates back to 600 AD and is still popular as an art form. Stencil dyeing is known as *Katazome*, and stencils are referred to as *Katagami*. *Katazome* involves placing a cut stencil over cloth, then applying a glutinous rice paste-resist, or *nori* (seaweed), over it. When dry, the uncovered areas are hand-dyed. This method allows for repeated or continuous patterns to be produced.

Katagami were traditionally made in Shiroko, near Ise, and the specialist craft is still practised there, in the traditional manner, to this day. The stencils were usually made of *kozo* (rigid sheets of mulberry fibre), and waterproofed with *shibu* (persimmon juice). Once the design had been cut, the stencil pattern was covered with adhesive or varnish and webbed with silk threads or human hairs, in cross-hatch, to reinforce it. Then, a duplicate stencil was glued to the original, making a rigid stencil sandwich. After drying, it was hung in a smokehouse – producing a stencil that was extremely durable, and tolerated repeated use and rinsing without warping.

These knife-cut stencils have a characteristic flowing line, and sometimes, after the paste-resist dries, the cloth is brush-dyed so that the colours flow into each other. This causes a misty, blurring effect which is known as *bokashi*.

JAPANESE TEXTILE

The Japanese were among the first civilisations to use decorative stencilling. This fine example of a stencilled kimono dates from the nineteenth century.

Stencils were used in dyeing from the latter part of the Muromachi period (1333–1568). The earliest example – a *katabira* (hemp kimono), with a *komon* (small dot) design – is said to have belonged to the military leader Uesugi Kenshin. Stencil dyeing became well-established in the Azuchi-Momoyama period (1568–1600). By the Genroku era (1688–1704), technical development was rapid. Along with the rise of the merchant class, the demand for komon-designed kimono cloth grew.

India, Persia, and Siam

Stencilling was used from around 600 AD in India, Siam and Persia. Siamese remnants show that, generally, flora and fauna were used as patterns. The designs were pinpricked, and the colour pounced through the holes.

In India and Persia similar methods were employed, although the subjects differed greatly: the Persians used sacred stories; the Indians geometry. Indian craftsmen were always in search of the perfect design, as they believed that this was the only way to spiritual advancement.

EUROPE

Stencilling travelled from Asia and the Far East via the trade routes to Europe, particularly Italy and France. Early evidence of this is the fact that many European leaders used stencilled designs as signatures on important documents, from the sixth century onwards.

Stencilling continued to gain in popularity throughout Europe over the centuries, and was used on furniture, church walls, wallpaper and textiles.

Italy

In Italy, during the early Christian era, stencilled letters were used to teach children how to read. And stencils were used by painters to transfer preliminary sketches for 'fresco' – a technique for mural painting – utilising the same basic pin-prick method employed by the Chinese in the Caves of the Thousand Buddhas, but combined with plastering. Fine white plaster was spread over the rough, mortar coating of the wall or ceiling. A preliminary drawing was stencilled with powdered charcoal onto the wet surface, using a sheet of paper that had the outlines perforated with a pin. The artist, following the stencil marks, painted on the moist surface with pigments derived from colours quarried in northern Italy – reds and yellow ochres, and blue from lapis lazuli. As the plaster set the paint dried with it, and a chemical reaction fused them together.

France

By the Middle Ages stencilling was very common in France, and was used to decorate everything from playing cards, games and books to textiles and wallpaper.

Wood engravers and colourists of paper sheets (papiers peints) were called dominotiers; the papers they produced were dominoes. From the end of the fifteenth century to 1850, dominoes were used for religious pictures; banners imitating draperies (carried by the devout on pilgrimages); songsheets; political squibs and newspapers of the day; as well as for decorative prints for the home. A peasant could buy a box of dominoes - twenty-five 30.5 × 42 cm (12 by 16½ in) sheets – and place them end to end to dress a fireplace, or make a wall border.

By the middle of the seventeenth century Rouen became the centre of wallpaper production. The first wallcoverings to be produced were flocked wallpapers with a raised, textured pattern. This was achieved by applying glue through a stencil to establish the design, and then rubbing over it with pieces of shredded wool. However, the quality of the paper produced was poor.

Around 1688 stencils were used on wallpapers designed by Jean Papillon, who was known as the 'father of wallpaper'. His son, J.M. Papillon, wrote a treatise on wood engraving which stated 'The only thing printed on this sort of paper is the outline of the design which is engraved on wood. This means of putting colours by stencil with a brush always produces a certain untidy result'.

Northern Europe

The major application for stencilling in Germany was in the area of screen printing fabrics, from the 1870s onwards. Other Northern European countries had long folk traditions of painted stencil decoration on walls and furniture.

AMERICA

From the late eighteenth century, stencilling became the main decorative technique used by settlers on the east coast. There was no link between the progression of design in this area and the developments in Europe, because the settlers were so detached from fashionable European influences. Decoration started as spatter painting, and progressed to more elaborate, repeat stencil designs.

The settlers decorated all aspects of their interiors – from household items to walls, floors and windows. Country images were popular, and included baskets of strawberries, plums, apples, beehives, birds – or any visual interpretation that would bring images of summer indoors, and help them to forget about the severe winters. A favourite motif was the pineapple, which symbolised hospitality.

As the popularity of the art grew, a band of roving craftsmen emerged to meet the needs of a growing population.

Theorem Paintings

Stencil pictures became popular, particularly on velvet. This folk art form of stencilling was known as theorem painting, because of the formulated manner in which designs were separated into groups or units. It became a fashionable practice among young ladies of the time, and by 1830 it rivalled embroidery as a finishing school skill, and was taught as part of the curriculum. Still-life subjects, such as fruit and flowers, were the most common, and frequently embroidery stitches and painting were mixed together in the same design.

The painting was constructed bit by bit, and each unit was traced onto thin paper that had been treated with linseed oil, dried thoroughly and strenghthened on both sides with varnish. Watercolour mixed with gum arabic was used for the stencilling, and after the paint had dried the details and finishing touches were applied by hand.

Floors

Stencilled floors were common almost until the Civil War period (1861–5). The technique required an expert to measure out the design accurately, and during the eighteenth and nineteenth century most families who could afford to do so

THEOREM PAINTING

So called because of its logical construction, theorem painting was a favourite pastime of fashionable young ladies of the early nineteenth century.

STENCILLED ROCKER

Many American chairs were embellished with stencilling of natural subjects like golden fruit, flowers and leaves.

numerous books on antiques, reported that old rag carpets were rejuvenated by being coated with filler and several layers of paint, and decorated with bright, tulip leaf and geometrical designs. He describes floorcloths as ' sailcloth built up by application of a starch filler on both sides of the canvas and then painted in patterns'.

Furniture

One significant pioneer in this field was Lambert Hitchcock, who started a factory in Connecticut in 1826, and employed one hundred men, women and children to make and decorate chairs. The backs and legs of the delicate, yet sturdily built chairs featured stencilling of fruit, flowers and leaves, burnished with copper and gold metallic paint. All bore the inscription : 'L Hitchcock, Hitchcocksville, Connecticut, Warranted'.

Seth Thomas was another manufacturer who utilised stencilling, in this case for decorating clocks. Whilst many others were instrumental in encouraging the development of stencilling on all types of small domestic items, ranging from jewellery boxes to trays.

Textiles

Stencilled bedhangings, counterpanes and tablecloths were also to be found in American homes around 1825. Usually, they consisted of brightly coloured designs in green, yellow, blue or red, stencilled onto homespun cotton. On some, the stencilling was touched up later by freehand painting.

Painted window shades were another form of stencilled decoration carried out by itinerant peddlers. The shades were made from fine textured muslin which was stretched, given two coats of size, and rubbed with pumice stone until smooth. The stencilled outlines were established by dusting a pricked-out design with a pounce bag containing pulverised charcoal, or by painting through a paper stencil.

Walls

Stencil designs soon found their way onto

employed a professional housepainter to carry out the work.

Others painted their own floorcoverings, and these floorcloths were at the peak of their popularity from the middle to the end of the eighteenth century. Stencilled versions did not appear until the nineteenth century.

In 1890, Carl Dreppard, author of

the plaster walls of homes. Both the vogue for stencilled walls and the actual designs were carried from village to village by journeying decorators. Their stencils were usually of leather or stiff paper, and their colours dry powder – which they mixed with skimmed milk from the farms.

One famous itinerant was Moses Eaton. At his home in Harrisville, Dublin, New Hampshire he stencilled patterns all over the walls. These were divided, by vertical lines of diamonds and petals, into nineteen panels decorated with flowers and geometric figures, while a band of roses and leaves ran along the chair-rail. Between two front windows he stencilled a flower-filled wicker basket in green and red, and a swag-and-bell frieze. His kit of stencils and brushes was found in the attic of his house. A total of 78 stencils were found, which made up forty complete designs, varying in size from weeping willows to small hearts, diamonds, and circles. He made clever use of his stencils, and by cutting a bevelled edge on the heavy paper ones he was able to produce sharper outlines. He depended solely on his eye and the top straight edge of the stencil for accurate positioning on the wall, and he used thick green, red and yellow paint.

Other documented examples include the home of Josiah Sage, in South Sandisfield, which also reveals extensive use of stencils in all rooms. Designs include vines and berries, swirly flower motifs, and entire panels decorated with baskets of fruit.

However, hand stencilling gradually declined as the mass production methods of wallpaper and carpet manufacture were introduced, but stencilling did survive as it was adapted for machine use.

Art Nouveau to the Present Day

Louis Comfort Tiffany, son of the founder of Tiffany, Young & Ellis (later Tiffany & Co) was a great influence on American stencilling of the Art Nouveau period, and is best known for his work with glass.

Tiffany used bold forms and loved strong, rich colours. He stencilled glass, borders and floors and occasionally entire rooms. His concepts and patterns were used over and over again in private homes and public buildings throughout the 1920s and 30s.

Until 1940 most homes would have had a stencilled border around the ceiling or edges of the wall. But, as decor became simpler in the 40s, stencilling largely died out, only to reappear again 20 years later.

BRITAIN
Medieval England

Stencilled decoration in medieval England was widespread, and it is documented that Henry III (1207–72) was fond of green walls scattered with stencilled gold stars. Unfortunately, few stencils have survived the centuries. Most were made from animal pelts or oilcloth, and have deteriorated. One lead stencil, the Meaux stencil – unearthed at a Cistercian Abbey in 1933, was presumed to be of medieval origin because of its rosette design. The diameter of the rosette itself is approximately 70 mm – about the size of an average rosette in thirteenth and fourteenth century painting. This is the only example of a painter's stencil known to survive from this period.

At this time stencilling was used mainly to decorate the walls of churches. But by the fifteenth century stencils were used in ecclesiastical decoration to imitate rich, gilded brocades. This was achieved by applying a gluey varnish to plaster and wood, through a stencil, and then powdering it with gold or heraldic coloured pigments. Popular designs of the period were stars, fleur-de-lys, suns-in-splendour, and the monograms prevalent in churches. Stencilling on the nave roof of Holy Trinity Church, Blythburgh, Suffolk is dated at around 1420–40. The design includes the monogram IHS, as well as floral motifs, and was stencilled on a white background, with scrolled traceries, painted freehand, in

EARLY MOTIFS

Stencilled decoration in Britain dates back to the thirteenth century. One of the earliest examples is in the Church of St Mary's, West Walton.

a shade of green. At the Hospital of St Wulstan, Worcester, a medieval painting of St Michael weighing souls was discovered in the 1930s; whilst in West Stow Church, Suffolk, a stencilled, oak panelled screen was found, featuring foliage designs, and dating from the first quarter of the fifteenth century. Few fifteenth century examples of stencilling have survived, but drawings and engravings suggest that stencilling was used in domestic as well as institutional buildings of the time.

Tudor and Jacobean England

By Tudor and Jacobean times, geometric designs were used to decorate larger manor houses. Simple designs were built up from squares and diamond shapes, and more complicated designs were composed by reversing stencils from panel to panel. There is a fine example of late sixteenth/early seventeenth century stencilling of this kind in the Colchester Museum, where a painted pattern simulates panelling, with cartouche shields in the centre of the panels. The main part of the stencil is 'in situ' at Josselyns, Little Hokesley village, near Colchester. A similar example can be found in a wall painting at Royston, Hertfordshire, where stencilled representations of pilasters alternate with Renaissance panels drawn freehand in black and white.

However, the use of stencilling diminished during the sixteenth century due, in part, to the disapproval of the Painter-Stainers' Company of London (a guild still in existence today), who described it as 'a false and deceiptful work and destructive of the art of painting being a great hinderer of ingenuity and a cherisher of idleness and laziness in all beginners in the said art'.

Nevertheless, decorated papers were stencilled to imitate the cloth tapestries and brocades used to furnish wealthy establishments, and these became increasingly popular amongst ordinary folk. At first they were produced in woodblocked squares, and used to line drawers and

niches. Then, 3.6 m (12 ft) lengths of stencilled papers were joined together and applied to entire walls.

The Seventeenth Century

It is not known how widely stencilled wallcoverings were used in London prior to the mid-seventeenth century, as The Great Fire of 1666 destroyed most hangings. But some examples from other parts of the country are still in existence.

A fragment of stencilled wallpaper, from the Old Bell Inn, Sawbridgeworth, Hertfordshire (circa 1700) is on display in the Victoria and Albert Museum, London, along with later examples.

The Eighteenth Century

Flocked wallpapers were the next significant development. Instead of gilding or

SEVENTEENTH CENTURY WALLPAPER

This fragment shows woodblock printing in combination with colours applied by stencilling.

coloured pigments being stuck to the stencilled design, powdered wool shearings were used instead. Stencils were also used as a means of printing a basic block of colour, so that woodblocked designs of birds, fruit, and flowers could be applied on top. However, this process disappeared as soon as craftsmen became skilled at creating single, elaborate, stencilled designs. An outstanding example of this can be found in the Tree of Life design, dating from around 1740, with its panels standing 1.9 m (6 ft 4 in) high.

The popularity of stencilling in the 1700s was due, at least in part, to the tax situation: plain paper had been dutiable since 1694, but in 1712 an Act was passed imposing a duty on paper that was

'printed, painted or stained'. At the time, wallpaper consisted of small single sheets, and although makers took to joining them into 11 m (12 yd) lengths, they had to be printed separately. Therefore stencilling was a much cheaper alternative.

In the eighteenth century, wooden floors were frequently left bare because it was believed that carpets were unhygienic. Such floors were often stencilled, and authentic examples can be seen in the Chapel Drawing Room, Belton, Lincolnshire and in the dining room at Crowcombe, Somerset. Both of these examples incorporate heraldic symbols.

The century also marked the introduction of tinted papers. Colours were added to a printed outline, and were usually applied by hand or stencil. Also, stencilling was extended to the decoration of books. Some eighteenth century choir books had music, text and decorations produced entirely by stencils.

The Victorian Era

Wallpapers were not produced in continuous rolls until the nineteenth century. In 1835, the Official Report of the Excise Commissioners stated that on every piece produced, costing 2s. 6d, duty was to be 1s. 3d. Consequently, wallpaper was too expensive for many people. Stencilling was much cheaper, as it could be carried out by the home-owner, a local plasterer or a house painter. But wallpaper became cheaper than stencilling in the mid-nineteenth century, as the tax was removed (in 1861) and mass production became possible.

Papers were recommended for use in all the rooms of the house, with the result that stencilling, generally, moved out of the home and back into churches and chapels.

During the early Victorian period stencilling was considered a suitable occupation for the amateur artist. After the Great Exhibition of 1851, decoration in the home featured medieval and

Japanese influences. These were reflected in stencil patterns during the late 1870s, which were frequently adapted from medieval tiles and Japanese textiles, as well as the Moorish works of Spain, with the result that many designs featured birds and flowers. Stencils were usually run at dado level on a natural background (a typical base being sage green or 'sober' yellow), but with brighter colours, such as red or mauve, incorporated into the stencilling.

One of the major references to stencilling at this time was W. and G. Audsley's work 'Polychromatic Decoration as applied to buildings in the Medieval Styles, 1882'. The book was intended, primarily, to show what could be done with stencilling, and featured coloured plates of the popular gothic style of the period.

William Morris

Morris was one of the great influences of the Victorian era. There is evidence that he used stencils, as they were made for him by Leach of Cambridge, a firm of local decorators, but there are few references to his actual use of these stencils. Some experts believe that his wallpaper for Jesus College, Cambridge is stencilled, others have doubts. Morris did undertake a stencilled

ceiling in the drawing room of a villa in Bromley, designed by Ernest Newton. He used a scarlet pimpernel pattern in buff, green and pink.

Gothic Revivalists

Most Victorian architects practiced stencilling to some extent, but perhaps the most gifted of the Gothic Revivalists was William Burges. Burges' principal works include the interiors of Cardiff Castle and Castell Coch, South Wales. Both Lord Bute's and Lady Bute's bedrooms at Castell Coch – their hunting lodge – incorporate geometric stencils in the wall decoration, while the arched ceiling of the Banqueting Hall is panelled with rich cedarwood and pine that has been stencilled all over with a pattern that is distinctly medieval in flavour.

Burges was fascinated by the thirteenth century, and this is reflected in his designs. In his own house at Melbury Road, Holland Park, London he decorated a room with stencils based on butterflies.

The Art Nouveau Movement

William Burges was instrumental in using stencils as a decoration for furniture, again with a medieval influence to his designs. Notable in the use of stencils as a decora-

WILLIAM BURGES

The work of Gothic Revivalist William Burges decorates the walls and ceiling of Lady Bute's bedroom, Castell Coch, Cardiff, and shows French, Gothic and Moorish influences in combination with pure fantasy. The theme is undoubtedly Sleeping Beauty.

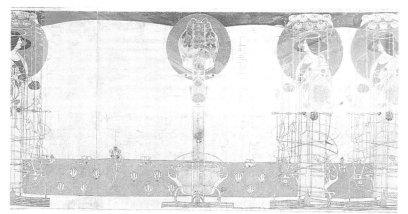

MACKINTOSH STENCIL
*Scottish architect, Charles
Rennie Mackintosh stencilled
these impressive panels at Miss
Cranston's Buchanan Street Tea
Rooms, Glasgow.*

tion for furniture was Charles Rennie Mackintosh, an architect from Glasgow. Characteristically, his pieces were tapered from top to bottom, and decorated with floral carvings, stained glass or stencilling. Frequently, he worked on painted wood, and many of his stencils featured Japanese-inspired motifs, or designs adapted from Celtic ornament.

Mackintosh often worked in conjunction with the Glaswegian interior decorator, George Walton. Between 1896–7 they created the Buchanan Street tea rooms, where Mackintosh executed impressive stencilled wall panels.

The Edwardian Era

The popularity of stencilling continued well into the Edwardian era, with many designs in the 1890s echoing the Art Nouveau style. Curved lines predominated in stencilled borders, and there was an abundance of natural symbolism with the use of leaves, insects and flowers, particularly tulips. Trade decorators were often called upon to stencil a frieze using these motifs.

The Modern Painter and Decorator by A.S. Jennings and G.C.Rothery was the main reference work of the time. Published in three volumes, in 1920, it included a chapter on stencilling, an art 'that deserves more attention than it usually receives'. It recommended the use of cartridge paper, linseed oil and a very sharp knife. At this time stencils were held onto the wall by means of specially made pins. Usually, distemper was used, though sometimes oil paints were preferred. Spraying through stencils was advocated as a means of saving time, graduating colour and preventing seepage under the edge of the stencil.

The Thirties and Beyond

As the war years approached, stencilling faded as a method of decoration, but now, in the 1980s, it is enjoying a revival. One contemporary influence, who is certain to make a lasting impact, is Lyn Le Grice, who creates stencilling masterpieces from a few cans of spray paint. It is not merely the skills she has that make Lyn a true artist of the craft, but also her appreciation of the subtlety of colour, with thought and respect for the fabric and character of the homes she works in.

Stencilling, like any other art form, progresses with time, but in order to preserve its traditions and history it is vital that the craftsmen of today can reproduce techniques of old. It is thanks to skilled conservationists and restoration experts that we are able to enjoy a decorative technique that originated so many years ago. Some of the best examples of stencilling in Britain can be seen in museums, stately homes, historical buildings and churches.

EXTERIORS

Stencilling doesn't have to be restricted to the inside of your home – house exteriors and gardens offer considerable scope for the craft.

Any stencilling outside needs to withstand the elements, so it is best to use oil-based paints. These are suitable for all surfaces, but do have the disadvantage of a slow drying time. Therefore, it is wise to restrict yourself to a few colours, or the job could take days to complete. It is possible to use emulsion or quick drying, acrylic stencil paint, but then the stencilling should be sealed with an exterior varnish, which will yellow it slightly.

As for a suitable surface, better results are achieved on a smooth background than on a roughcast or pebbledash finish. When stencilling on top of a gloss coat it is essential to rub down the area first, sanding through the stencil, in order to provide a key for the stencil paint.

PAINTING OUTDOOR WALLS

In a shady corner where plants refuse to thrive, or on a boring, brick or rendered wall that needs a facelift, stencils enable you to brighten a bleak outlook. You can create a classic garden, with stately pillars and urns, or a charming cottage flowerbed, complete with old fashioned roses and dancing delphiniums.

Some companies make lifesize stencils of balustrades and pots, shrubs and trees, but if you want to create large flowers you will probably need to cut your own stencils. In such a case, it is easier to copy a design from a flower painting rather than a photograph, as the simplification of line probably will have been done for you. Flowers with bells or spikey petals are particularly successful, and are at their best facing forwards, to show off their stamens.

Bear in mind that a large scale stencil isn't always essential. Borders only a few inches deep can look wonderful on exterior walls, especially if you choose a geometric or architectural design (see page 18).

EVERGREEN TREES
An ordinary back yard is transformed into a stylish patio by this lifesize stencil of a balustrade, complete with orange tree urns. The addition of real flowers in a terracotta pot complements the illusion. Grey paint has been stippled sparingly onto an exterior wall to produce a mottled stone-like effect. Stencil paint was used on this occasion, as the position is fairly sheltered. The colour should survive many wet seasons before it starts to fade.

CREATING ORIGINAL HOUSE SIGNS

CLASSIC PORCH

A plain porch is given a classical air by appropriate stencilling. The
architectural border on the walls is a commercial stencil, and was selected to
echo a moulded trim on the front door. The laurel wreath and numerals were
hand-cut in a complementary style. Note how the three-dimensional effect of
both the border and the numbers is achieved simply by the clever arrangement
of thick and thin lines.

A hand-painted house sign looks particularly impressive, and is a good starting point for stencilling outside. No artistic skills are necessary to produce a chic sign when you can stencil. All that is required for a professional finish is careful measurement, to ensure that the figures or letters are central and level. If you are not confident enough to paint directly onto the exterior wall, door or gate, it is a good idea to use a wooden plaque, which subsequently can be fixed to the appropriate surface.

First, select a style of lettering. A selection of stencil alphabets, including numerals, is available from art suppliers. It is important to choose a typeface that is in sympathy with the architecture of the building. If your home is modern, stick to one with straightforward, clean outlines. For a period property choose a more ornate script

Also, bear in mind the place where you intend to site the sign. First stencil a sample on paper so that you are able to measure the width to make sure it will fit. Then cut an appropriately sized piece of new wood, about 1.25 cm (½ in) thick, and round off the corners with sandpaper. Measure your sample lettering, and mark the wood with a pencil to establish the central position. Varnish the stencilling before use.

You should follow the same procedure if you want to work directly onto the wall of the house – first checking the stencil is vertical, by using a plumb line or spirit level.

You might wish to incorporate a stencilled picture into the sign, such as a solitary flower, or a bird. Alternatively, portray the name of the house visually. If you are lucky enough to live in Rambling Rose or Pear Tree Cottage you are likely to find a suitable design amongst the range of commercial stencils. More obscure titles will need home cutting (see page 115).

EMBELLISHING PATHS AND PATIOS

Nothing makes a garden look more dreary than a sea of grey concrete. But, if your budget doesn't stretch to smart paving stones, you can disguise an ugly concrete patch using a stencil.

It is a good idea to map out the design onto squared paper before you start. Books on early decorative detail are excellent sources of reference for flooring styles. Some of the popular patterns of the late seventeenth and early eighteenth centuries can look deceptively modern, and work well with properties of more recent periods. Experiment with different shapes and tones to achieve interesting optical effects. For example, darker areas will advance and lighter areas recede, to give a strange feeling of perspective.

Once you have planned your design,

divide the area up into shapes. The size of the shapes will be governed by the overall area: narrow paths, for example, will look best with just two of the same tile across the width, whereas patio-sized areas will take a greater number of much larger squares. Cut a strip of stencil material the length of one paving stone, and about 3 mm (⅛ in) wide, and use this to outline the 'stones'. Finally, lightly dab on paint within these lines, using a sponge, to achieve a subtle, stone-look effect.

When stencilling on the ground, it is essential to use a paint which will withstand all weathers, as well as constant traffic. Emulsion will work, but will eventually flake unless thoroughly sealed; oil based paints are best, and for concrete use special colours (see page 120).

PAVEMENT ART

Unsightly concrete slabs take on the appearance of colourful terrazzo flooring with the help of a stencil. It was essential that the decoration would withstand constant traffic, so chlorinated rubber paint was used. This has excellent exterior durability and, amongst other applications, is used for road markings. The paint was applied in two coats, with darker shading over a lighter base, to give a weathered look.

DECORATING OUTSIDE WINDOWS AND DOORS

WINDOW PELMET

Framing a window top and bottom with a shaped pelmet and window box not only improves the visual proportion, but also provides a canvas for creative stencilling. Here, a flutter of butterflies amongst summer flowers adds country charm, and provides much needed colour when winter comes. In order to achieve a degree of realism the creatures' wings have been painted in azure blue, russet and golden yellow.

Wide windowsills are perfect locations for window boxes, and a stencilled panel on the box front adds to the colourful effect. If you don't wish to buy or construct one, stencil onto a plank of wood, of suitable size, fix it across the front of the sill, and then slip some plastic pots behind it.

If your window would benefit from a cheerful look, but the sill is too narrow either for a windowbox or for flowerpots behind a stencilled plank, then stencil a fake box. Paint the box onto hardboard and add stencilled flowers, starting with shorter ones at the front and taller varieties in a row at the back. Make the back blooms a solid mass of colour, with no white spaces showing, so you can cut around the outline shape quite easily with a jigsaw. Varnish the finished plank thoroughly, then attach it to the wooden sill by fixing a piece of wood to the back and screwing it down. If the sill is stone or cement use a two-part epoxy resin adhesive, specifically meant for outdoor use.

It is unlikely that you will be able to extend your stencilling onto the window frames. This is because the woodwork is usually fairly narrow, and therefore the stencils will be so small they will not show. Even on wider frames the shaped mouldings make stencilling difficult.

Doors, however, offer plenty of surface area for stencilling. Garage doors are great fun to work on, and it is worth trying to make an impact by making up a large, stencilled mural from separate sections of material. For example, try a lifesize bicycle leaning against the door, or the front of a Rolls Royce emerging from within.

It is advisable to restrict yourself to one or two colours, and use a large stencil brush to speed up the task. Make the stencil up in sections, using notches to register each part of the design (see page 115).

If you can't face tackling a project on this scale, then stencil onto a smaller door. For example, add a trompe l'oeil copy of your

DECORATING GLAZED DOORS AND GLASS PANELS

favourite newspaper, dated the day of stencilling, peeping out from the letterbox on your front door.

Coloured glass panels are often found in period houses, either set above the front door as a fanlight window, in a decorative stairwell, or as a landing window. They serve the dual function of letting in light, and at the same time retaining privacy. If your house has lost these features, plain and simple panes can be given the stained glass treatment with a stencil and glass paint. For inspiration look at books on Art Nouveau and Art Deco designs. To make the staining look even more authentic, outline the stencil with plastic leading.

DOUBLE GLASS DOORS

Exotic jagged leaves, stencilled on the glass with an airbrush, take on an engraved effect. Designed by Julia Roberts, the tongue-shaped leaves suggest tropical undergrowth and provide a link between the inside and outside of the house.

BEAUTIFYING GARDEN BUILDINGS

Sheds and garages lend themselves to outdoor stencilling, most having at least one plain wall. Try trailing a climber up some stencilled trellis. Fake the flowers as well, or combine both, so when the real flowers fade the painted variety behind are still in full bloom.

Painting on preserved wood

On sheds, hutches, bird tables and any other wooden garden pieces, it is impor- tant to find out what wood preservative they have been treated with before you start decorating. You cannot paint directly onto creosoted wood, although some other preservatives will take paint on top. Check for instructions on the container. Howev- er, if the wood is new and untreated, you may be able to experiment by stencilling with wood dyes, and then sealing with a clear preservative on top.

PAINTING GARDEN ACCESSORIES

PLANT CONTAINERS

This group of stencilled pots would look just as good indoors as they do in the garden. Special bisque stains were used, because they adhere well to all kinds of pottery and do not require re- firing. They were applied fairly thickly, to compensate for the porosity of the terracotta, and the stencil was held in place on the curved surface with masking tape. Lastly, the pots were given a top coating of ceramic spray sealant as additional protection against the weather.

If your patio provides a site for container gardening, consider christening some of the plain plant pots with a splash of paint. Beginners should tackle a trough to start with – straight sides are considerably easier to cope with than the curves of cylindrical pots. The thinner acetate stencils lend themselves to working around a curve, but the thicker versions are more difficult to use, and novices will find working with oiled card on a curve virtually impossible. Check the area under the rim of the pot to make sure the size of the design fits. Also, you should test the surface with paint before you start: try a sample patch on the base. Ceramic paints are suitable for work-

ing on terracotta, but should be applied sparingly. However, the best medium is bisque stain, which adheres very well and does not scratch off. Some pots come ready-sealed, but the cheaper, uncoated kind are extremely absorbent and tend to soak up the paint, resulting in a fuzzy edge to the stencil. With these it is best to apply the paint using a small cosmetic sponge, or an artists' sable stippling brush. Unless, of course, a soft edge actually enhances the design, as in the illustration of the cat (opposite). Finally, add a protective coating with a spray sealant.

Stencilling in the garden doesn't have to be limited to troughs and pots. Try decorating your rubbish bin: stencil it with a bold banana skin, a collection of cans or packets. Brightly coloured aerosol sprays are by far the best medium for this type of project.

The most effective stencilling ideas for gardens are often light hearted. For example, you could paint a bucket and spade frieze around the children's sandpit, or decorate the dog kennel with a hessian sack, scattered letters and the torn trouser leg of a fleeing postman – it might discourage burglars!

STENCILLED SEAT

Simple deckchairs look stunning with the addition of stencilled summer flowers. It is sheer scale that creates the impact here; the exaggerated blooms fill the whole seat. The fabric paint is stencilled heavily, in order to show up against the deep-dyed canvas fabrics. Revamping chairs in this manner is an inexpensive way of acquiring a set of original garden furniture.

HALLS, STAIRS AND ENTRANCES

When it comes to interior design, the space behind the front door is perhaps the most forgotten part of the home. Inevitably it becomes the parking place for bags and bicycles, and the most convenient spot for storing coats, umbrellas and boots. In fact, the main entrance should be thought of first in your plans for home decorating. It acts like the opening chapter in a novel – setting the mood and creating a link with the sections that lead off it. The problem with most halls is that because there are so many doors concentrated in a small space, there is very little wall left to decorate. But bear in mind that you don't need much wall area, if any, to make an impact with stencils.

GRAND ENTRANCE

Towering columns and trellis panels add architectural interest and complement this spacious stately hall.

Stencils on the wall are useful to counteract the disjointed feel so often caused by an abundance of doors. Paint your stencil to skim along the skirting, and up and around each door frame. Then, if appropriate, make it follow the staircase up to the next floor, or run it into an adjoining room.

CHOOSING THE RIGHT STENCIL

Deciding on the appropriate style of stencil for a hallway is often a more difficult choice than for other areas of the home. Being rather like a 'no man's land', an area that is always passed through rather than lived in, halls seldom have an identity. Consequently, the priority when decorating an entrance is to maintain a flow – any stencil used in a hall should relate to the overall ambience of the home, or at least to the scheme of the main room that leads directly off it.

In a house where the style is primarily contemporary, and which is furnished with blonde wood (limed oak or ash) furniture of slender lines, with dhurries spread over the floor, a simple geometric stencil in cool or sharp colours, like black, yellow or grey, would be suitable. Where furnishings are on the traditional side, and feature rich woods like pine, oak or mahogany, and fabrics such as chintzes, velvets and oriental rugs, choose a busier stencil, with rounded shapes painted in warm colours like brown, cream or red.

By using one stencil it is possible to relate a hall to a neighbouring living area, even when the colour scheme is vastly different. The same pattern carried from one room to another will accentuate continuity. Carry through the design, gradually adjusting the colours by changing the tone, or dominant shade, as you progress around the corner. On the other hand, if you would like a different mood in the hall to the living room, choose a stencil that looks good used either way, and turn the motifs upside down in one of the rooms, whilst maintaining the same basic colour, but introducing a new, secondary shade of it. This will give a very different look, but the two rooms will remain related.

STENCILLING ABOVE A CORNICE

Colleen Bery filled the space between picture rail and cornice with a floral design that can be appreciated at eye level whilst descending the stairs.

MOCK MOULDING

Gaby McCall sprayed on white auto paint, followed by ivory and beige on top to give depth and perspective.

CORRIDOR OF LILIES

Lengthy corridors with endless wallspace, but little room for furniture, are ideal for creative stencilling. Verona Stencilling lined this one with railings inspired by cast iron mouldings. The giant pot of lilies adds contrasting shape and colour, and the border on the ceiling, adapted from a carpet design, echoes the curves of the railings.

ALTERING PROPORTIONS WITH STENCILS

PERSPECTIVE STENCILLING

A stencilled trompe l'oeil mural by Verona Stencilling cheers up a poorly lit passageway. The chequered tile floor creates an exaggerated impression of perspective, and the sense of space is enhanced by the use of soft, speckled dark grey and blue tones alternating with mottled cream. The shimmer of metallic paint gives the urns a realistic bronzed appearance, and the static terrace is brought to life by a solitary peacock and two drifting ivy leaves.

To take full advantage of stencils, you should examine all their possibilities whilst planning your scheme. Try varying the position of the stencil to change the proportions of the room. If you paint a border at chair-back height you will produce an instant dado effect, a technique that reduces the cavernous impression created by a towering ceiling, and makes the space more cosy and inviting. Equally, adding a large, stencilled motif in place of a missing cornice in a spacious, high ceilinged hall will help to bring the eye down and create a more friendly atmosphere.

Another technique is to run a border, at a low level, along the top of the skirting board. This will visually lengthen the space. If your hall is extremely narrow you can give the impression of width by using stencilled squares on the floor, and painting them in various colours, to give the effect of a diagonal pattern.

Dark stairwells and endless passages, so common in apartment blocks as well as large, old houses, can be both claustrophobic and tedious. Stencilling is the ideal way to break up the monotony of long narrow corridors. The best approach in this situation is to stencil a large mural along the walls, as small borders will get lost in such a vast space.

A brightly coloured background is usually necessary to compensate for poor light, but this can create a rather 'hospitalised' feel. If you want to soften the glare but keep the predominantly airy feel, try sponging a pale, warm colour, like dusky pink or buttermilk, onto the surface, and then stencilling on top of this background.

A progressive, pictorial stencil that 'moves' with you as you walk along is fun. Try a few fallow deer gambolling along, or a fox being pursued by a pack of hounds – culminating in his escape.

WORKING ON WOOD

Decorated doors leading off a hallway can look extremely effective, and are a good way of pulling the area together and making it more akin to a proper room. Consider how you use the hallway before you embark on stencilling the doors. If the doors are left open most of the time, choose a design that coordinates with the hall decor, but won't clash with the schemes in the rooms that the stencilled doors lead into.

Panelled doors are ideal for stencilling as the mouldings provide convenient ready-made frames. Floral sprays look particularly pretty in the centre of the panels, but you'll need to hunt out designs of the correct proportions that work in the space; many commercial stencils are designed primarily for use as borders, and others may be too big. If you find it difficult to buy a ready-cut design that is suitable for use as one single motif on a door, you can always adapt a flowing design by using individual flowers from it, and reversing some of them to build up a posy, and then finishing-off with a bow. Work on one side of the stencil first, and clean it before turning it over, or you are certain to end up with smudges.

Plain flush, wood doors tend to look rather dull, but they can be given some character quite simply by painting and stencilling. You could even create the illusion of panels by stencilling an architectural design that stimulates wooden mouldings. Be sure to use a slightly darker shade of paint within the 'panelled' area in order to give the impression of depth.

Emulsion (latex) paint provides the best base for stencilling, and is recommended for sameday painting and stencilling because of its quick drying time. Stencil on top using more emulsion, acrylic-based stencil paints or sprays.

Gloss-painted doors are tricky to work on and are best repainted in emulsion or, if a hard-wearing finish is essential, satin or eggshell paint. Failing this, the most practical approach for stencilling directly onto gloss paint is to tape the stencil in position and then rub through the design using fine sandpaper. Sanding provides a key for the stencil paint to adhere to. It is essential to use an acetate stencil for this, as the card variety tend to tear under abrasion. Final sealing with polyurethane is advisable (just coat the decorated area by repositioning the stencil once more).

Don't use aerosol paints if you are a beginner or if you are working on gloss woodwork. It takes considerable practice to acquire the spray technique, and it is best to attend a course run by an expert. The fact that the sprays are cellulose-based means that they could react with an unsound gloss finish, causing the surface to bubble and rise.

One way of avoiding paint compatability problems is by stencilling on stripped doors. This is particularly effective when combined with folk stencilling, which seems to go hand-in-hand with stripped wood. It is important that the design and the colours have a country mood. Choose subtle tones: autumnal shades like rust, gold and damson that will blend into the mellow wood. Alternatively, work in woodstains so the completed stencil takes on a marquetry look. Try out various colours, using them sparingly. Always remove all traces of grease and wax before you start, and remember that any woodwork that is exposed to the knocks of family life will need the protection of a few coats of polyurethane.

Stencilling is a clever way of emulating the old-style doors with engraved glass panels. You can paint a convincing etched glass effect by stencilling with white glass paint. Avoid borders for this look, but build up a picture that includes various

DECORATED DOOR
Stencilled sweet honeysuckle borders this landing ceiling and trails down the walls to different levels either side of the door frame. In addition, it is twisted vertically and used to decorate the panels of the door. The panels were rag rolled first with cream paint, to provide a broken background for the stencilling.

PAINTING STAIR RISERS AND TREADS

If your stair carpet has seen better days, investigate the woodwork beneath. It may be worth removing the covering altogether, and stripping the paintwork back to bare wood so that you can stencil the risers. Alternatively, the staircase could take on a new lease of life with stencilling on freshly painted risers. Salvage any good parts of the carpet, and use them on the treads, tucked and tacked firmly under the front edge and back of each step.

COUNTRY STYLE DOOR

Whether this front door opens into a country or city home, the stencilled baskets on stripped pine give it a definite rural stamp. Aerosols have been used here by an inexperienced stenciller, and although the effect is pleasing a few first time errors are in evidence: the palette is limited – for a better result build up the final colour from a range of shades, rather than using one direct from the can; there is a hint of overspraying, which contributes to the solidity of colour; and the outline is indefinite because the stencil slightly lifted during spraying.

leaves, flowers and scrolls.

Using a small stencil brush and a delicate stencil, you can reproduce another traditional craft by decorating some door furniture with stencils in such a way that the result looks hand-painted.

To achieve this hand-crafted look you must use a stencil that has been cut without bridges (see pages 114–15). Choose charming floral designs for finger plates, or stencil single flower heads onto door knobs (pulls). It is wise to use enamel or ceramic paint for china door furniture, and then to seal it so that it does not scratch off (see page 120). Finally, don't discount painted door furniture for a modern setting. It fits in quite well if you choose the right style: just substitute a more graphic floral, or a simple geometric, for the traditional naturalistic garlands of flowers.

If you want to forego carpet altogether, there is no reason why you shouldn't stencil the treads if you protect the paintwork properly (see page 31).

Stencilled spindles and hand rails have a definite appeal, and are evocative of Swiss chalets or painted canal barges. To achieve this effect you will need to choose a stencil that has a small motif and is made of plastic, to enable manouvreability around the curved surfaces.

WATERWAY STAIRWELL

This winding, cottage stairwell resembled a scene from Wind in the Willows once stenciller Gaby McCall had finished work. Gaby, who learned her skills from Lyn le Grice, uses auto sprays and prefers to work on a broken painted finish. Here, the walls were sponged with green on white.

The wealth of pondside plants and creatures were researched to ensure that they would look convincing, although artistic license was used to make them fit the space, and colours were changed to improve the visual quality. Subtlety of colour was achieved by overlapping sprays and mingling several shades – seven greens and a pinky colour make up the foliage. There is an awareness of light and shade, with dark colours concentrated at the base of the leaves and paler ones at the tips. Similarly, the ducks flying in the distance were oversprayed with white to make them lighter than those in the foreground.

STENCILLED STAIRCASE

Bands of stencilled butterflies on the risers suggest that a patterned carpet runs up this staircase. Carefully examine the undergrowth on the wall to spot the same butterfly hovering over a flower. The stairs were given three coats of eggshell paint to ensure an extremely tough surface underfoot, whilst providing a excellent base for Gaby McCall's spray painted stencil.

MANOR HOUSE HALL

This grand, Jacobean manor house hallway sorely needed some form of wall decoration above the mellow oak panelling. A border stencil of fleur de lys and star shapes, adapted from an old family crest carved in the staircase (see right) provided the answer. Amber colours were used to echo the golden glow of the wood and the sandy floor tiles.

DECORATING HALL FLOORS

Stencilled floors can look stunning, and are immensely practical in high traffic areas such as halls. Rent an industrial sander to strip the floorboards back to their original state. Then stencil a border around the edge, or a pattern over the entire area. Seal wooden floors with at least four coats of polyurethane varnish, thinning each down with one-third white (mineral) spirit, and lightly sanding down between each layer to key the surface for the next coat.

Parquet flooring makes a good base for stencilling, although with herringbone patterns you must make sure that the stencil doesn't conflict with the directions of the wood blocks.

If you find a wooden floor too noisy or draughty, old vinyl flooring can be revitalised with paint. Three coats will be sufficient to cover a previous pattern. Then stencil the design, and follow up by applying two coats of polyurethane varnish to protect your work. On all stencilled floors, sand down and re-apply a fresh top coat of varnish every year.

Before deciding on how to stencil your hall floor, first consider its shape. Stencilling an all-over geometric pattern will be most successful if the hall is fairly square or rectangular, and is without any nooks or crannies, alcoves, or narrowing corridor areas, such as are typical at the side of a staircase. If this is the case, use a stencilled border instead, running it near the edge, and following the contours of the hall.

If you are short of ideas for floor designs, refer to books. Patterned floors have been in favour for centuries and there is no better way of reproducing them than by stencilling. Try out shapes on paper first, before you start cutting out stencils. It is possible just to cut one or two stencils and get plenty of variations by altering their arrangement, changing colours and combining different stencil components.

A TASTE OF EGYPT
This entrance was given an Eastern flavour, using stencils derived from Egyptian wall paintings. The two areas either side of the archway were pulled together by embellishing the window blind with heiroglyphics and the arch with trompe l'oeil pillars.

FLOOR BORDER
This flowing leafy border, designed by Lyn le Grice, is derived from a wood carving on the stair supports. The muted greens have a natural feel that blends comfortably with the mellow pine boards.

LIVING ROOMS

Stencilling can play an important part in living areas by cleverly co-ordinating disparate elements into a complete scheme. Before you decide on colours, bear in mind that a north-facing room will benefit from warm tones, whereas a south-facing room can take cooler shades.

BORDERS EN MASSE

A combination of borders divides the walls of this sitting room into panels. The variety of scale and direction works primarily because the striking colour combination – deep french blue warmed with rich terracotta – is carried throughout the scheme. This sense of integration is reinforced by the use of the same stencil design on the floorcovering as on the walls, and the repetition of the trefoil motif on the coffee table.

SELECTING SUITABLE STENCILS

FRUIT BORDER

A harvest festival of fruit strung along the ceiling of this passage provides an introduction to the dining room beyond, where the individual fruit stencils are overlapped and piled up to make a basket arrangement. The stenciller, Paul Treadaway, has taken great care to blend the colours with the surroundings – picking out the shades of the curtain fabric, the brickwork and the wooden door.

BASKET DETAIL

The basket has been copied from an antique silver wirework basket. To avoid cutting five separate stencils, Paul cut five masks and laid them in turn on top of the original stencil when working on each colour.

It is important to choose a stencil that you feel comfortable with. If you are hesitant about what to choose, play safe by taking a design from a favourite possession like a rug, a piece of porcelain, a treasured lamp or a fireplace tile, and then you will be unlikely to tire of it. Fireplaces themselves make a good starting point, offering several small-scale stencilling possibilities. You could stencil behind the mantel shelf, onto a plain wooden surround, or even onto plain tiles on the hearth. However, the hearth tiles should be painted only if their function is purely decorative. It is not advisable to paint them if the grate is in use – unless you use an on-glaze paint that is fired-in (see page 120).

With flower-strewn furnishings already in the room, you may be wary of using additional flowers in a stencil, but, if you choose a stencil that echoes their shape, regardless of the type of flower, the two will mingle well. If you can't match the flower shape with a pre-cut stencil it is far better to cut your own, rather than choose another conflicting shape.

Always look at the features in the room – there may be a moulded ceiling rose, or some carved wood on an old cupboard that will spark off an idea.

MIX AND MATCH STENCILLING

Most of these stencil designs by Colleen Bery are variations on the same ribbons and flowers theme; cleverly adjusted and added to so that they are appropriate for each object. All harmonise perfectly, from the be-flowered cushions to the grey sponged coffee table, which features a rather more graphic Egyptian lily. The ash tiled floor has been given a colour-washed finish. Colleen applies signwriters' paints with a very dry decorators' brush, gently stroking a little paint on, so that the colour is absorbed into the grain.

CREATING AN INTEGRATED LOOK

In a country-cottage-style living room, furnished with oak, cherry or pine, the most appropriate stencil would be small with rounded shapes, probably a floral design, or one incorporating hearts, and would be best used to emphasise architectural features such as pretty windows, sloping ceilings or character doors. If the flavour of the room is primarily 'country', but nevertheless has a grand air, a stencil on a larger scale, and of a more dramatic design would be most apt, and should be used all over the walls, sponged on to give a softer effect (see page 119).

In a 'city' environment, where hard, glossy surfaces like glass, lacquer and chrome are prominent, the room would look better embellished with a classic, sophisticated stencil. Try a geometric motif, perhaps in one colour, and use it selectively – possibly on a light fitting, or above the fireplace.

However, there are few restrictions when stencilling. The effect of a stencil depends not so much on the specific design, as on the colours you use and the extent to which you use it. Take a classic, curvy shape, stencil it in blue and gold, and it will contribute to an Art Nouveau look in a traditional living room. But if you use the same stencil, omitting some of the shapes, and paint in grey and black, then it will take on a much more contemporary feel. *You* dictate the mood evoked by the stencil according to how you use it.

MARRYING OLD AND NEW

Room planning from scratch is rare – most of us have existing furnishings to work around, especially in the sitting room. The eternal problem of marrying up old and new is easily overcome by introducing a stencil, and combining elements from both in one design.

You can combine a new, geometric upholstery fabric with existing floral curtains by simply pulling out one of the more striking shapes from the window fabric design. Set the motif in a band dotted to look like the texture of the sofa fabric, and then take the stencil around the walls as a border.

When making some changes to a living room, stencilling can help bridge the gap. If, for instance, you are changing the paintwork but maintaining the furnishings, trace a stencil design from the fabric and sponge it onto the wall, thereby subtly linking old and new. Again, look at the fabric carefully and pick out one part of the design which has a good outline yet is not particularly dominant: it might be a small bird among the flora, or a border incorporated in the print.

Discontinued lines need not present difficulties when you are capable of stencil cutting. If you have an extra window that needs dressing, but the original fabric is unavailable, you can make up a co-ordinating blind using a complementary stencil. When you intend to run the stencil along the bottom edge of a made-to-measure roller blind, it is worth ordering the blind to include a deeper piece of fabric beneath the batten, to allow space for a painted decoration (see page 78).

The problem of matching frequently crops up when a wall is knocked down, and two previously separate rooms become technically one. Painting stencils around the walls provides a speedy means of visually tying together the two areas.

EVERGREEN ROOM
Here, the walls of a glass-roofed extension have been stencilled, by Gaby McCall, with an abundance of plants, in order to create a conservatory feel. Artistic licence has been used to combine jasmine leaves with an uncharacteristic twisted trunk.

COLOUR-WASHED ASH FLOOR TILES
This fine, stencilled floor is laid with square, ash tiles and features colour-washed stencilling by Colleen Bery. She favours this translucent effect, produced by applying diluted paint, which allows the natural wood grain to show through. Here, in this sunny dining area, stencilling in shades of silver with a zing of lemon gives an impression of Mediterranean living. The contrast with the floor shown on page 40, where the same basic geometry is used, is considerable. And although the colours here are much paler the surface is just as practical, being sealed with no less than five coats of lacquer.

ADAPTING AND INTEGRATING FIXTURES AND FITTINGS

It takes a great deal of pluck, and a strong wrist, to sentence a sound, but dull, wallcovering to the scrap heap. The easy options are to live with it, paint over it in white, or simply put up with it until you can summon up enough energy to scrape it all off! Stencilling, however, is a simpler and more satisfying solution. You will even be able to get away with leaving the furniture in the room while you work.

PASTEL SITTING ROOM

The use of a powder blue stencil design on a multi-coloured background makes a refreshing change from the conventional approach of mixing several shades in one stencil motif set against a plain coloured wall. The embroidery-like design is borrowed from the blind (detail page 66), and is garlanded at dado level to highlight features in the room. Accessories have been given the stencil treatment too: a stencilled picture hangs in the corner, whilst a dhurrie rug introduces a more graphic design which nevertheless merges happily with the floral theme.

It is preferable if you can paint onto an existing wallcovering that is a plain, pale colour. This presents very few restrictions on your choice of stencil. However, papers with a small pattern or a delicate design

can be greatly enhanced: try a contrasting border of a larger version of the pattern. Alternatively, you could experiment with a neat, punchy geometric design, set against a floral background; or with a splashy floral border over a striped paper.

Whatever scheme you opt for, it is important to try out the colours first on spare paper (lining paper will do). Temporarily fix this in place with a low-tack masking tape, to assess the colour 'in situ'.

It should be noted that when working over relief or embossed wallpapers, greater care should be taken: stipple the paint on gently, to avoid crushing the raised pattern.

Wallpaper isn't the only problem feature that can be given new life by stencilling. Take a look at how you use your living room – is there a door that is never closed, even in winter? You might consider removing the doorway completely, replacing it with an arch, and then highlighting this new feature by stencilling all around it. Fireside alcoves can be given the same treatment: round off the top with a forming arch set into plaster, paint, and finish off with a stencil. You should choose a stencil with a soft line, and one that will adapt to the shape of the archway. A hard, angular edge will look clumsy set around a curve.

Also, stencilling is a clever way of visually splitting-up different parts of an open-plan living area. For example, around a dining table you might use a stencil all over the walls, skirting and furniture to create a well-defined, cosy atmosphere, then on the walls surrounding the sofas you could use the same stencil, but restrict it to running at dado level. Use stencilling on a hard floor to achieve the same effect: using two colours in your design throughout, but varying the combination. Or, you might care to make up a border around a rug, or use a chequered design to circle the table.

It is important not to isolate functional

living room fittings from the rest of the decor. So, before you automatically paint all woodwork gloss white, consider the alternatives. Satin paint gives a more subtle sheen than harsh gloss, is available in a wide range of colours, and provides an excellent surface for stencilling. Dragging or sponging a coloured emulsion onto a white base will also give a softer appearance (see page 124).

Use the same paint effect on the radiators as on the walls – even if that means extending a skirting level stencil across the radiator. You will have to tape the stencil down carefully for this, to make sure the brush does not slip over the ridged surface.

Follow the same principle at the top of the room: if necessary use pelmets to disguise a difference in the level of windows on the same wall; or to link open alcoves to adjoining walls.

DECORATED FIREPLACE
Strawberry plants trailing along this fireplace add a touch of originality to plain, unadulterated pine. Clear, coloured stencil paints have been used here for bold contrast, but for a softer more subtle effect, that merges into the wood, use stencil crayons or spray paint. It is advisable to remove any wax from wood before stencilling.

DECORATING STUDIES

A home office is perhaps the area where modern and traditional furnishings are combined most often. It is not uncommon to find a modern, functional desk installed in a Victorian or Edwardian house, or an antique mahogany or oak desk in a modern home. In these circumstances, a lively decor that creates a stimulating environment is far more important than the actual style of the stencil used. So stay away from soft, relaxing colours and introduce instead a splash of something a little more vibrant. Keep the basic decorations fairly muted, but then add colour using bright, desk accessories and a few bold, stencilled motifs. However, it is a mistake to make the stencil too busy, as this may prove distracting.

GRAPHIC DESIGN

A rather offbeat stencil is a dominant feature in this study. Extraordinary not only because of its combination of shapes, but in the way it is composed on one small section of wall. The room is used as a home office by the graphic designer who originated this design, which focuses on a cluster of irregular shapes tumbling from the light source and intersected by two vignettes of light. The impact is heightened by the contrasting Pacific blue venetian blind.

TROMPE L'OEIL BOOKSHELVES

The bookshelves in this impressive study/library are seemingly packed with weighty tomes. In fact Paul Treadaway has used six stencils in various combinations to produce 65 trompe l'oeil books. The background was first painted in VanDyke brown acrylic, then the books and pictures painted on top, using shades of acrylic mixed with emulsion. The lettering on the spines was applied freehand in a golden yellow paint, by a professional calligrapher; stencilled letters appeared too 'hand made' for the purpose. The sphere base and the temple were given a granite look by brushing on the base colour, followed by several colours speckled on top with a natural sponge. The sphere was marbled through the stencil by taking off wet paint with a damp rag to produce a mottled base, then adding veins with a feather dipped in paint.

DRAMATISING DINING ROOMS

INSPIRED BY A CLASSIC GARDEN

For a dining room floor with a taste of the outdoors, Colleen Bery took an aerial view of a formal garden as her inspiration, and dotted favourite garden flowers such as wisteria, old roses and bluebells amongst the geometric shapes. The bold design and strong colours work well next to simple yet elegant furnishings.

Dining rooms are, by their nature, more envigorating surroundings than sitting rooms, and will take a dramatic, stencilled effect quite happily. 'All-over' designs are ideal, though they require considerable forethought. You should assess the amount of light in the room before you set to work with the stencil brush. In particular, be wary of stencilling panels en masse, with no breathing space in between them –

they can be overpowering in small, dark rooms, though they can look sensational in spacious areas.

If in doubt, start by leaving double the stencil width between each band, so that there is room to fill in gaps later on, if necessary. If you don't feel brave enough to tackle the entire room, you could always restrict yourself to a stencil that will work on one whole wall, either by arranging the motifs to make up an overall pattern, or by building up a mural from pictorial stencils.

In a dining area that is a frequent venue for dinner parties, use stencils to reflect a moody, intimate atmosphere. Metallic paint can look stunning, especially under the flicker of candlelight. Try gold on cream walls, or silver on midnight blue, and opt for an impressive theme, such as fiery, Chinese dragons. Spray paints are an effective way of getting instant glitter.

WALLPAPER EFFECT

Here, soft shades of lilac-blue and candy pink are contrasted with a punchy geometric stencil design, by Nicola Wiehahn. And the stencil-framed abstract bird over the fireplace helps to make this dining room stylish, dramatic and very individual.

KITCHENS

Kitchens are the hub of the household and most of us spend more time slaving over a hot stove than we care to admit. Everybody deserves a well-decorated kitchen to cheer them through their chores.

Decorating a kitchen requires thorough planning. It is crucial that a working kitchen is practical and safe, as well as pleasing to the eye.

Stencilling a kitchen makes a lot of sense, as it is a convenient way of introducing some colour and pattern, whilst retaining easy-to-care-for painted surfaces.

Streamlined, no-fuss kitchens, with no trimmings at all, can be clinical and cold. Stencils, used selectively, will add character to this type of scheme without spoiling the underlying simplicity.

ALL-OVER STENCIL

Stencilled daisies scattered over the wall maintain an element of simplicity in this streamlined kitchen/diner, and contribute to a sunny summer atmosphere.

CHOOSING A STENCIL

Choose a graphic stencil, and do not over-use it, when a hi-tech style is the order of the day. There are a few commercial borders made up from basic shapes, such as triangles, which would be suitable for a modern kitchen. Use them in silver and black to echo stainless steel and cast iron cooking equipment. If there is no room for a border, scatter a few bold motifs at random between the wall cupboards and worktop – a plump red tomato or bold yellow corn have particularly good shapes for stencilling.

Alternatively, restrict the stencil decoration purely to accessories. Try painting some glossy red cherries onto plain glass jars, using glass paints (see page 121). Or make original bookends for the cook-book shelf from two pieces of wood fixed at right angles, and decorated with a stencilled pair of chefs' hats. You could stencil a plain tea cosy with a slice of chocolate cake; or liven up a plain, open shelf by attaching a stencilled continental style fabric border trim, depicting a row of coffee mills, for example.

FISH DETAIL

Two leaping trout rising to the bait look particularly lifelike, and make a perfect wall decoration in the cosy kitchen of 'Trout Hollow' cottage. The three-dimensional effect is achieved by careful shading of the skin in tones of silver, green and pink, although the texture of the woodchip wallcovering contributes to the overall scaley effect. The paint is stippled onto the body, with black lightly brushed on top, and dragged over the fins and tail to give the impression of movement. The entire project took just twenty minutes to stencil.

CHOOSING COLOURS

The colours you decide to use for stencilling can influence the entire style of the kitchen, irrespective of the design of the motif. For example, take one stencil, such as a basket of flowers. If you try it out in red, on a piece of white painted wood, it is almost certain to conjure up a Tyrolean mood. But alternate this red basket with a basket in emerald green and the kitchen will have more of an Italian ring to it. Start again with blue on white, add a checked border below, and the look becomes decidedly French *paysan*. Splash yellow or vivid pink into the design and the kitchen will take on a more frivolous character, and if you are after a traditional, English country kitchen style keep strictly to neutrals like oatmeal, biscuit and cream.

CREATING A CO-ORDINATED LOOK

SUMMERY KITCHEN

Stencils have been used here to extend the bright atmosphere of the adjoining sun-room into the kitchen. Squared timber trellis stencils, over windows and openings, are combined with diamond shaped stencilled panels running down the wall, kitchen cabinets, and through to the tiles.

Stencils make colour scheming easy. There is no need to scour the shops to find a fabric to match your tiles, or tiles to match your fabric. Cut a stencil instead. This is a particularly useful way of revamping the kitchen, especially as the choice of manufactured co-ordinates is considerably more limited for this room than it is for the bedroom or living room.

There is no limit to the inspiration for designs in the kitchen. Look out for food illustrations on calendars, jar labels, cookery books and magazine features; for pictures of herbs, spices and wild flowers try seed packets. You could make a simple stencil shape of pots and pans. Or simplify the structure of a woven wicker basket and, using fabric paint, sponge it onto a blind hanging in a window recess. Then make a border from the shape of the basket rim, and, using a suitable paint, run it around the window frame.

In other words, just look around and use your imagination.

PAINTING CUPBOARD DOORS

There is nothing sacred about kitchen cabinets. Don't be afraid to try painting them. Like any other fabric of the house, they will benefit from a fresh look. You will need a large stencil for cupboard doors. Before you begin stencilling you must remove the wax or varnish from the cupboards, using a proprietary product. And after stencilling you should re-seal them. Take time selecting the colours to be used on natural woods – you will be better off steering clear of the brighter ones, and sticking to the more muted shades.

When working on white door fronts, consider stencilling in one colour only, but varying the tones to give depth and perspective. Plastic laminate units can be painted too: first key the surface with wet and dry paper, used wet with plenty of soap as a lubricant, and then use an eggshell finish, rubbing down between each coat.

Choose an acetate stencil to work on any coving, as the flexibility of the plastic makes it more suitable for bending around the concave curves.

Tongue and groove panelling is perfect for a kitchen, where it serves the dual purpose of being a convenient way of adding extra insulation and of cutting down on condensation. In addition, it offers superb scope for stencilling. Try leaving some planks undecorated: stencil every other one in small kitchens, every five in larger rooms. Keep the design cottagey by selecting a trailing floral display and stencilling in subdued shades; or create a Scandinavian look by using bronze colours – butterscotch, caramel, or even cherry red on pale, natural wood. Make this style more interesting – and authentic – by giving the wood a limed look first: just rub watered-down white emulsion (latex) paint into the wood grain (see page 121).

If cladding the entire room doesn't appeal to you, then introduce panelling on a smaller scale – use it to replace a hardboard cupboard door, or pin it to a frame around a sink or boiler to disguise ugly pipework.

DECORATING PANELLING

Another fruit theme used for a kitchen, but this time with a classic approach. The ripe strawberry, complete with a tiny flower springing from it, was designed by Pavilion for a special commission, and was inspired by a popular French medieval symbol. This example demonstrates the effective, yet little practiced, use of scattering one stencil.

MATCHING STENCILS WITH CHINA

CO-ORDINATED STENCIL

A charming floral ring, adapted from a favourite Villeroy and Boch dinner service, fronts these chic, painted Smallbone cabinets.

Few things look prettier in a kitchen or kitchen dining area than a display of gleaming china. Use the design and pattern of your dinner service as the inspiration for a stencilled decoration on the wall, table linen, chair cushions, or a frill to edge some plain curtains. To achieve a realistic embroidery look, outline stencilled flowers onto the edge of a tablecloth, using special broderie paint. This gives a raised embroidery effect when pressed on the reverse side with an iron (see page 79).

On the other hand, if you have a favourite fabric design that you would like to make a feature of, buy some cheap white china and copy the design onto it using ceramic paint. But first check that the design will convert to a stencil: intricate patterns should be avoided as they are fiddly to cut out, and aren't as effective as strong, bolder shapes. If you intend to use flowers, single blooms are better than bunches, given the relatively small area available for decorating.

Also, bear in mind that no paint applied on top of a glazed surface will be permanent unless fired (see page 121). So decorated china is best kept for display, or occasional use followed by careful washing with no rubbing or scouring.

DISGUISING UGLY FIXTURES

Most old kitchens have their eyesores. If it is not the bulky boiler that is too efficient to swop for a new slimline version, then it is a maze of pipework, or the old refrigerator that has seen better days but insists on staying alive. However, all these items can be rejuvenated with a stencil.

Box-in old pipes with a sheet of hardboard or wood, and then paint and stencil. Stencilling directly onto pipework is usually rather tricky, because it is difficult to work around a curve in a restricted space. But do remember that nobody is going to examine this sort of stencilling very closely, so errors won't be as noticeable as they would be on a wall or floor. Appliances, on the other hand, are best tackled with aerosols. Auto spray paints will withstand the heat of an engine, so obviously they are suitable for working on a boiler. First remove any panels you can, and stencil them out of doors in order to cut down on the fumes. As an added precaution, wear a builder's gauze mask. When you start to work on the immovable bits, make sure you cover surrounding cupboards, walls and the floor with newspaper, as the fine paint spray is difficult to control and tends to stray. You will find that bolder designs work best on these types of fixtures and fittings.

FRUIT SALAD

Here, stencilling is used to camouflage an unattractive but essential appliance. The bunches of fruit add a splash of colour and an element of fun to an otherwise mundane corner. A bendable plastic stencil made it possible to decorate the curved flue pipe; whilst auto spray paint was used on the boiler, as it is suitable for metal surfaces and can withstand high temperatures.

PAINTING TILES

TROMPE L'OEIL

Stencilled platters rest on top of the wall cupboard (above), whilst the ceramic tiles are equally unreal.

DUTCH STYLE KITCHEN

The charming children playing were, in fact, stencilled onto plain floor tiles using ceramic paint, and sealed with varnish.

Replacing tiles in the kitchen is a major and expensive task that usually involves removing the too firmly attached old tiles, cleaning off bits of adhesive from walls, and some re-plastering. Painting the existing tiles is a far easier alternative. After cleaning with a mild fungicide solution, undercoat the tiles or paint them with an eggshell finish. Then apply stencil paints, as usual, and finish with one thinned coat of polyurethane varnish. Use a gloss varnish if you wish to replace the sheen and make them look like commercially available tiles (see page 122).

It is also possible to stencil onto new, satin tiles, but it is important that they are of a good quality, and that they have been thoroughly fired – especially if you intend to re-fire them after stencilling. Some imported tiles have imperfections in the glaze, and therefore should be avoided. If you plan on re-firing use 'on-glaze' enamel to stencil (see page 121). However, you can use ceramic paint, sealed with polyurethane.

EMBELLISHING FUNCTIONAL ACCESSORIES

Hanging space for the essential batterie de cuisine is a bonus in a kitchen – it saves frantic searching through drawers for the right tool at the right time. Put up some pegboard, the old standby hanging system, and stencil the silhouettes of the tools onto the board so you know where to replace each piece of equipment. For a more attractive hanging system, use a slatted wooden rack, stencilling alternate slats

with, for example, a pretty, countrified floral motif.

Finally, no kitchen is complete without a pinboard: make a basic one from cork tiles, mounted in a frame, and use border stencils to mark up the board into different sections, so that information for local events, important telephone numbers, invitations, shopping reminders etc are easily located, and not buried beneath other items.

SPOT THE STENCIL

There is more stencilling around this kitchen sink than first meets the eye. Wheat is an appropriate motif for the curtain. The design on the tiles is made up of four chaffs of wheat, and some of the objects hanging from the pole aren't in danger of gathering dust.

BEDROOMS

However conservative you are about decorating other rooms in the house, the
bedroom is the place you can afford to indulge your fantasies and to splash out
on a profusion of colour. Special paint finishes (see page 124) are particularly
effective as a backdrop for stencilling.

FREESIA POSIES

Stencilled posies over the bedhead create a canopy effect, and add a rather regal
touch to this freesia-covered bed. The flowing ribbons link the wall, headboard
and quilt in a unified whole. Note how the use of shading where the stencilled
ribbon narrows creates the impression of twisting, and how the central posy on
the wall is made up of more flowers than the others, in order to balance the
overall composition.

SETTING THE MOOD

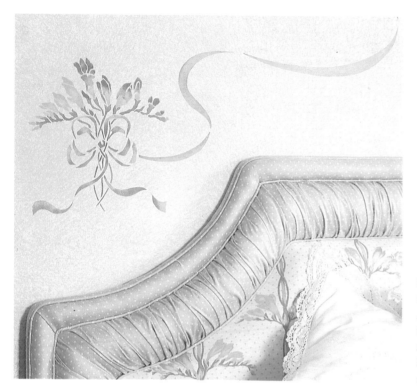

FOLLOWING THE BEDHEAD SHAPE

A single bunch of freesias tucks into the space above the sweeping curve of the bedhead, linked by a ribbon to the next motif.

If a pretty, delicate decor appeals, there are dozens of ready-cut stencil designs to choose from: ranging from little posies, to billowing ribbons tied up in big bows. The best way to achieve this effect in a bedroom is to make up a palette of soft but clear colours, reminiscent of summer flowers. Think of the sharp blue of campanula and the range of pinks in dianthus. Whereas, if you feel a muted impression is preferable choose faded shades, but spice them with a brighter tone occasionally.

For an even more striking look, avoid pastels altogether and use less predictable colour combinations such as lilac and jade, mustard and turquoise, or magenta and silver. Cut your own stencils with the emphasis on large, dramatic flowers, like chains of wisteria hanging from the ceiling, foxgloves growing from the floor, or a mass of bright scarlet poppies all over the walls.

If the room is large, and has ample light, consider painting it a chic, deep shade, like navy blue. Then stencil white snowdrops or gypsophilia on top, and set this off by using stark white bedlinen. You can extend this romantic look to the furnishings: a round table covered with a floor-length, flouncy cloth, stencilled to match, makes a charming dressing table. Alternatively, resurrect an old, kidney-shaped dressing table, drape it with stencilled fabric, and continue the stencil onto the mirror.

If your bedroom becomes your retreat when life gets hectic, you'll appreciate surroundings where you can lie back and escape from the world. For a tranquil environment, keep colours predominantly cool, with a hint of warmth brought out in the stencilling – lemon stencilled on ice blue, apricot on silver grey, or coral on mint green, are particularly effective.

DRESSING THE BEDROOM

SCANDINAVIAN STYLE BEDROOM

The simplicity of this attic bedroom, with its tongue and groove clad ceiling, suited an uncomplicated stencil treatment. The room was washed all over with the palest eau de nil, to provide a softer base than conventional stark white, and then stencilled selectively using variations on two basic designs.

Drapery anywhere in a bedroom adds grace and elegance, and you don't need an expensive fabric to achieve a stunning effect. Stencilling can contribute richness or prettiness even to the most mundane of fabrics. So be extravagant with window dressings (see page 86) – behind the bedroom door, detached from the bustle of family life, you can get away with full flowing fabrics.

Try generously arranging fabric around, behind or over the simplest of beds. You might cover a bed in ivory lace, and then cut out a stencil motif similar to the lace pattern. Stencil this onto cheesecloth, in a pale honey shade, and hang it from two curtain poles, fixed to the ceiling either side of the bed. Then stencil some pretty pillowcases, and hang plain fabric from a rail behind the bedhead. And finally, cut a length of fabric, stencilled in the same design as the pillows, and tie it into a flamboyant bow around the drapery. Or, for a really rich look, completely cover plain walls with a stencilled fabric, painted in a deeper shade of the plain background.

DECORATING CEILINGS

Where better to stencil a ceiling than in the bedroom. Flora and fauna are the obvious choice for a fantasy scene, or you could stencil a microcosm of the galaxy, to gaze at while you lie in bed. However, whatever you choose, it is advisable that you are well practised at stencilling before you tackle such great heights.

If you intend to stencil all over the ceiling, it is wise either to stick to one colour or, for a multi-colour effect, to stencil in bands or panels with a painted space in-between. When using several colours, limit yourself to one colour a day so that you don't suffer discomfort from a stiff neck – it can be quite tiring work!

A platform-type ladder is almost essential for stencilling ceilings. (With a standard ladder you will spend a considerable amount of time and energy running up and down it.) If you don't have one, use a sturdy workbench that can be moved easily from one area to another or a scaffold board between two stepladders.

Ceilings, like floors, require careful planning. Measure the area first, and work out a plan on graph paper so that the design is well proportioned. Then, draw this onto the ceiling with a hard pencil. There are two pitfalls that should be avoided. Firstly, don't plan a design around a central light fitting and assume it falls in the centre of the room. Secondly, if you decide to take the design (a band of flowers, for example) from the centre, across the ceiling to the four corners, and down the wall, it is very important that first you decide which side of the corner you want the stencil to continue on the wall. Measure the width of the stencil, and draw the guideline from the centre of the ceiling so that the edge, rather than the centre, of the stencil pattern meets the corner of the walls. If you don't do this, the corner will cut the pattern in two.

PANSY TRAIL

Chains of pansies cover this cottage bedroom ceiling like an overhead canopy of flowers. Each chain radiates from the centre to the edges, and continues down the walls. The stencil, comprising four individual sheets for each separate colour, was cut without bridges to give the painting a freehand quality, and echo the Osborne and Little fabric that inspired it.

WORKING WITH THEMES

FANTASY MOTIF

Two theatrical figures in exotic costumes dance over a bedroom ceiling. Around them stars, moons and urns sparkle like jewels against black velvet.

This one-off design by Eddie Anderson and Anne Glaskin of Pavilion, was an ambitious project: first the ceiling was given four coats of black emulsion; then scaffolding was erected, and the dancers completed by the stencillers whilst lying on their backs.

As we have already discovered, stencilling is the ideal way to carry a theme through a room. For example, you can transform an ordinary bedroom into a Japanese style room with just a little ingenuity, and a stencil brush. You will find many ideas for stencils in books on Japanese art. Start by painting the walls vanilla, and either buy or paint accessories in jet black.

The bed will play a central role in the room design. If you don't have a futon, a Japanese style sofa bed, settle for dressing up your divan in an oriental fashion: make it as basic as possible by removing any elaborate headboard; painting plain wooden ones shiny black; stencilling on a simple, oriental motif, in gold or red, and adding a natural colour duvet. When there is no bedhead, stencil the motif onto the duvet cover, and add some cushions – make some bolsters in natural calico, trimmed with black cord piping, and add some square calico cushions, dimpled in the centre by stitching with two lengths of coarse black thread.

Keep furnishings to a minimum, but if you are short of storage space, use a screen. It provides a convenient surface for hanging clothes, and is a handy way of concealing clutter in a corner. Make one up from a

wooden frame, and pin on taut fabric or strong Japanese paper (available from good art suppliers), then stencil it with just three bold motifs.

Finally, strip floorboards back to their natural state, and stencil on a black border to reflect the style of the bed, or scatter a few stencilled birds around the walls. But remember, the essence of Japanese living is simplicity of style, so beware of overdoing the stencilling. Choose only two or three sites to stencil, and leave it at that.

Bedrooms are a good place to indulge a passion for glitz and glamour. Mirrors, silk and slinky satin – anything that spells

LACE AND SATIN

The bone lace panel at the window was the inspiration for this delicate stencil design, scalloped around softly sponged walls. The cameos scattered at intervals are a clever way of adapting the border stencil into a different motif – one scallop has been flipped over and reduced in size to form an oval.

ART DECO DESIGN

A series of exaggerated arches echo Art Deco sunbursts. The stencilled border, helped by the soft amber glow, evokes a glamorous setting that would be well accessorised with a satin bedspread, covered with shiny, shell-shaped cushions.

FURNISHED IN SHADES OF BLUE

This chic bedroom, decorated by Verona Stencilling, illustrates how effective spray stencilling in one colour can look. Fifteen different shades of blue were used to achieve these results.

The stencilled hanging shelves and the Chinese mural were inspired by Chippendale, the gate below the dado adapted from a fretwork chair and the pictures within the frames were copied from the front of a lacquer chest.

CHINESE CURTAINS

A collection of Chinese plates and pots stencilled onto coarse cloth make an unique pair of weighty curtains. Verona Stencilling used auto spray paints for this project, so the fabric requires specialist dry cleaning, although the colour is likely to fade each time.

opulence – are prerequisites. Quilted beds-preads look the part, and stencilled fabric takes on an extra special quality when the stencilled sections are padded and outlined in stitching. It takes time and skill to produce a professional-looking, quilted cover such as this. The easiest way of getting good results is to cut the fabric to size, stencil, and then stitch around each motif. Quilt by slitting the fabric behind the motif, and padding it with polyester filling (see page 89).

If you would prefer to keep your bed-linen 'easy-care', use a simple, white rib-bon-trimmed duvet, and make a feature of the head of the bed. You could fix a mirror behind it, and stencil around the edge with glass paint, or decorate the frame with stencil paint. Alternatively, you might sten-cil some fabric, and make it into a padded headboard by quilting it in the same way as the bedspread, or just stencil directly onto the wall behind the bed – but remember to position the stencil so that it isn't hidden behind the pillows.

There are many other styles to choose from. A modern, fresh look can be achieved by leaving the walls plain, and introducing checked fabrics against a painted floor. You might stencil a basket of red apples, criss-cross trellis, or trailing ivy around the edge of a white painted floor. Seal it with polyurethane for protection – this will yellow the paintwork slightly, but not enough to adversely affect the appear-ance. Striped fabrics can look very chic: stencil plain cotton by sticking lengths of wide tape along the fabric, and painting over the top with fabric paint. (Lay the tape along some carpet first, to remove any excess stickiness). Combine various-sized stripes together for visual interest: for a bedroom chair cover paint narrow stripes onto a fabric, and run a fine, linear stencil between them. Or, paint broad stripes down a wall, and stencil a geometric band between each stripe.

STENCILLING STORAGE

A fair amount of space needs to be re-served in the bedroom for storage. A quick and inexpensive alternative to built-in or freestanding furniture is to turn alcoves into useful hanging spaces. Put up a roller blind for a neat finish and then stencil the front of the blind to co-ordinate with the rest of the decor. Or, when you've built in cupboards, treat them like the walls. Paint the doors the same colour, and then stencil in the same design. This way you will create a greater sense of space in the room. Alternatively, apply a dragged paint finish to the wardrobe doors before stencilling. This subtle lined effect can be tricky to tackle; the secret is to complete the run without stopping (see page 124).

ONE ROOM LIVING

When one room takes on several functions, a stencil is a useful tool to pull the different elements together. This bedroom is a classic example of how several stencils work in harmony. Garlands, wreaths, baskets and ribbons are all based on one basic shape – a laurel leaf and fruit. Suitably stencilled in autumnal hues, using auto sprays, they cover every item in the room – from cushions to cupboard.

Children's rooms

There is nothing children will love more than their own roomful of fun, and with stencils you can create the most fantastic effects. Also, stencilling is a cheap and speedy way of changing the decor to the craze of the moment – as friendly, furry animals inevitably make way for intergalactic spacemen.

Patience is not a characteristic children are usually noted for. Once the decorating starts they will expect to see an instant transformation in their room. The easiest way to revamp a room quickly is to use one of the ready-cut borders on the market and adapt it to your own design scheme. After all, a product sold as 'border' need not necessarily run in straight lines around the room, at just one level.

NOAH'S ARK
This biblical theme is an ideal subject for decorating a child's room. The charm of this stencilling stems from the immaculate fine detail cut into each creature, and the sensitivity of colour used – a soft blend of hues from the spectrum, emanating from the rainbow and rain droplets.

CHOOSING A STENCIL

There is a wide selection to choose from, ranging from rabbits to robots. You can use these characters to surround a window, to hold up a coat hook, or to edge the front of some shelves. What you can conjure up will depend on the individual stencil but, as an example, a group of juggling clowns could be turned into a human pyramid by leaving out the clubs and balls, and turning some of the clowns upside down so that they stand on their hands or heads. Similarly, you might stencil a pair of cartwheeling clowns, and run them at angles around light switches or door handles. Equally, by looking at the cut-outs in the stencil, you can make up patterns from the basic shapes, and use these to decorate furniture so that it mirrors patterns elsewhere in the room.

DUTCH PAIRS

Partners clad in clogs, linked in a line of hearts, make a pretty pastel border. One pair have been cleverly used as a picture, framed with flower heads and highlighted with bunches of brightly coloured balloons. The stenciller has shaded one side of the circle to give a spherical impression.

CHOOSING THEMES FOR CHILDREN

If you are prepared to spend a bit more time, you can create an entire fantasy world for a child's bedroom by cutting your own stencils. Usually, this is more successful if you combine stencilling with other paint techniques. For a space set: sponge the walls and doors grey and lay a rubber-studded floor covering to look like a bumpy, moon surface or stencil lookalike craters onto a plain, inexpensive rug by painting concentric circles, shading the centre one to give the impression of depth. Then stencil cosmic craft zooming overhead, on the ceiling, and circles of luminous paint, to look like planets. Stencil these circles in decreasing sizes, so that they appear to fade into the distance, and then shade one side, to

BONNETS AND RIBBONS

A young lady in her old fashioned frock makes a delightful picture on a little girl's bedroom wall. Her flyaway hat adds movement, and links up with the bonnet border above. Ribbons form an important part of Gaby McCall's design, featuring in the dress, trimming the hats and linking the two together.

give them a three-dimensional spherical quality. For a final touch, add a green creature creeping around a door frame, or slinking out of the cupboard door. If you would prefer not to cover an entire piece of furniture with little green men, compromise by squeezing a mini stencil onto the knobs (pulls), or hiding a baddie inside the top drawer – ready to leap out. You will find plenty of design ideas in comics and on toy packages.

Hobbies make ideal subjects for stencilling: paint a straightforward, stencilled mural of cricket stumps complete with bails, and a ball in flight on an adjacent wall; or make up a border of tennis racquets, footballs, riding hats or ballet shoes. You could combine stencilling and mural painting for a more varied effect (see page 88). Again, children's comics are an ideal source for both the ideas and the designs for your stencils.

THEMES FOR LITTLE ONES

For younger children, combine freehand painting with stencilling, and create a woodland scene, with wild animals hidden in the undergrowth. A vertical brown band, painted from floor to ceiling, will turn into a tree trunk with the addition of a stencilled squirrel leaping away from it, or an owl peering around it. Stencil leaves on the ceiling, directly above the 'trunk', and paint the skirting boards green, with spikey, grass blades growing out of the top edge and concealing more stencils – a black and white badger's head, or a red fox's tail, for example.

Also, nursery rhyme themes are always favourites. Humpty Dumpty converts into a simple stencil. Sit him on top of a mantle shelf, with the Hickory Dickory Dock clock above, the hands approaching 1 o'clock and the mouse running up the pendulum.

TEACHING WITH STENCILS

Stencilling is so simple that the children can join in too. Encourage them to cheer up some basic boxes for sorting out toys or shoes, or indeed anything that encourages them to be tidy! If you have more than one child, you will find a set of stencil alphabets invaluable for establishing the ownership of various objects.

Another good idea is to stencil cartoon-style characters onto a piece of natural cotton, turn it over, stitch the top and bottom into loops, thread wooden battens through them, and then hang it on the back of the door.

Alternatively, make a growth chart by stencilling simple pictures up the wall, or on canvas or wood, in one vertical line. Start at 70 cm (2¼ ft) from the floor and mark each 10 cm (4 in) interval with a stencilled picture and number. Then record the date, in pencil, as the child reaches each new stage.

Simple, blocked shapes are perfect for wall decorations as an encouragement to the child to identify and name new things. Make up a frieze of basic objects that are easy words to say, such as tap or cup. You could make a simple counting game, by stencilling a border of objects arranged in groups of twos, threes, fours and so on. Or paint a line-up of teddies, and give each a different coloured jacket to aid in colour recognition.

When painting animals you need not cut out your own designs. Instead, choose from a few commercial stencils of farm animals, or from a classic Noah's Ark set, complete with two characters and a collection of beasts, to make up a row of animals entering two by two.

PARROTS AND STARS

Stencilling is used in numerous ways in this child's room. An arched niche becomes a cage, with the introduction of a friendly stencilled parrot on a perch, behind bars of brightly painted dowelling. Stencilled labels on stacking crates encourage organised sorting of toys, and natural cotton has been stencilled with a cheerful pattern to make a hobby horse head. A continuous border would have been insignificant in this busy room; instead, stars outline just the niche and overhang.

CREATING AN ORIGINAL CO-ORDINATED LOOK

One of the most enjoyable aspects of decorating with stencils is the potential for creating an original co-ordinated look, by combining stencils with furnishings.

Black and white with a splash of scarlet or emerald makes a stunning scheme, and can suggest a speedway image teamed with the right accessories. Start with a succession of racing cars speeding around the walls; stencil a large meandering line on a hard floor to look like the track. If there are no floorboards or they are unsound, lay down sections of stencilled hardboard about 105 cm (3½ ft) square. In fact, these can be a better background for large designs, as the joins are less noticeable and further apart than floorboards.

However, it is the finishing touches that really make the idea work. Hang plain green curtains and make a flag pelmet similar to the one used in the nautical room opposite, and a duvet cover with appliquéd flags to match.

Use the same basic colourways and carry through a board game look, again extending the theme from the stencilling to the furnishings. Start with a stencilled rug or floor featuring giant black and white checks that function as a games board. Make black and white draughts by painting 24 similar-sized jar lids. To stack them easily when kings are won, use small pieces of sticky putty.

Complete the look by stencilling black dice or domino spots on white curtains, and suspending rope ladders that serve as handy clothes hangers and suggest snakes and ladders.

The effect that thoughtful accessorising can have on the success of a scheme is illustrated opposite. The lifebelt framing the stencil, the 'sail' drapes in beach hut stripes, and even the shingle-like flooring, give added weight to the stencilling and contribute to the nautical look.

STENCILLED WAVES

A dry brush was used for the waves so that the minimum of paint was applied. The stenciller worked with a circular motion to give an impression of the white spray of a swelling tide.

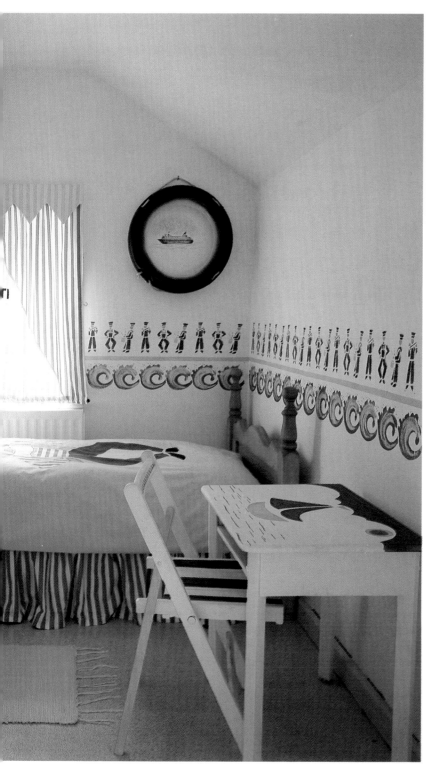

NAUTICAL THEME

This crew of jolly sailors brightens up a white wall in a little boy's bedroom, and sparks off the nautical theme. The basic border is a commercial stencil complemented with hand-cut swirling 'white horses' and a band of golden sand. All three are displayed at child's eye level for the benefit of the occupant.

The furnishings and accessories are an integral part of the scenario: a stencilled duvet features a giant hornpipe jigger, first stencilled then 'dressed' with an appliquéd shirt; a stencilled sailing boat decorates the painted desk, and a distant liner can be viewed through a lifebelt 'porthole'. The flapping sail-like curtains add the final touch.

COPING WITH TEENAGE ROOMS

CO-ORDINATED SOFT FURNISHINGS

An ordinary divan in a corner of the room was made to look rather special by embellishing it with a delicate sheer fabric, stencilled with the same trailing vine design as on the walls. The secret of successful stencilling is in evidence here: a design is used repeatedly, but with care; the use of the stencil along only one edge of the fabric lends it a style and individuality not found on commerically printed fabrics. Just a simple trim decorates the lampshade, but the cool seersucker duvet is left undecorated.

Teenagers achieve great satisfaction from devising their own room schemes, and by using stencils they find planning and decorating the whole room, from start to finish, more fun and less work. Whatever their taste, it is likely that they will want to furnish emphatically as a statement of their individuality.

Second-hand furniture that can be home-renovated is a good buy. Stencilling directly onto high gloss lacquer paint presents problems of adhesion, so if you want a lacquer look it is best tackled by painting a matte coat first, stencilling on top, and then adding the shine by coating with gloss polyurethane varnish. Japanese motifs are perfect for lacquered furniture. Whilst with stripped pine, woodstains look classy when stencilled using the simplest of classic shapes, to give the impression of marquetry.

Since teenage bedrooms double as entertainment suites, accommodation for friends is essential. Stencilling cotton covers for giant squashy floor cushions provides a cheap and colourful answer to comfortable seating. Large designs are advisable – avoid petite floral prints, as the combination of scales will look strange.

When rooms are shared, screens are ideal as a way of maintaining privacy and providing an extra wall for decoration. Glue cork into the centre of each panel for pin-ups, and add stencilled mouldings to neaten the edges. Alternatively, stencil all over the screen and use it to drape and hang clothes.

WINDOW FRAME

Inspired by an idea from Mark Hornak, dramatic ferns and fronds were stencilled around the window frame, to pick out the pretty ecclesiastical shape.

FRESH TEENAGE THEME

Stencils give teenagers the opportunity to express their individuality. Tanya longed for a fresh, green and leafy environment. In her loft room, parchment coloured paint provided a warm base, and a trailing vine was stencilled along the angled walls to emphasise the architectural form. Large, stencilled floor cushions act as informal seating for friends.

TEENAGE GRAPHICS

BLACK AND GREY TEENAGE THEME

Saleena prefers a more graphic style to Tanya (see page 64). Monochromatic tones of black, from silver and steely grey through to jet, were perfect for this.

CANE BLIND

A reverse stencilling design was produced by applying strips of masking tape in a bow shape, then spraying black paint over the blind.

The opportunity to spray the walls with what they please will appeal to most teenagers, and stencilling is by far the best way to make sure that the results are good. Innovative graffiti produced by spraying paint through stencils is a cult in France, and this popular artform can be seen embellishing subways and exterior walls of buildings. Existing examples come in all shapes and sizes, the subject matter varying from spiders to bicycles and can-can dancers, as well as silhouettes of megastars like Grace Jones.

STENCILLED FOUR POSTER

Stencilled ribbons and bows, in powder pink, entwine the turned posts of this
fairytale bed and pretty up a plain, pine chest. Single bow motifs are scattered
over the fine, white drapes for co-ordination.

BATHROOMS

CASCADING TULIPS

Borders needn't always run in straight lines. Here, tulips cascading down the walls make a feature of the window. The striped fabric and painted boards contrast with the floral design, whilst the edging tiles echo the flower head shape.

Usually, the bathroom is the most difficult room in the house to revamp. All too often what starts out as a few ideas to change the colour scheme, and give the room a new look, can turn into a major operation involving the replacement of ceramic tiles or the renewal of sanitary ware. By stencilling, the redecoration can be carried out not only at low cost but also with little upheaval. Furthermore, in bathrooms and loos you can afford to be bold with colour. Splash out on the shades you love, but would not dare paint in the living room. For example, you could combine slate grey with acid yellow, vivid geranium pink, bright apple green, or sharp raspberry red.

EMBELLISHING THE BATH

Stencilling is the ideal way to make the most of a coloured bathtub that you have inherited, but would not have chosen. For example, a primrose yellow bath can look insipid teamed with washed-out walls so try spicing it up by stencilling borders of bright blue bells. And a turquoise bath would be improved with a stencilled apricot trellis.

The bath itself is the best place to start stencilling, and there is always a way to brighten it up. Baths are continually exposed to the onslaught of daily toilette, and the enamel suffers by becoming chipped or scratched. There are various ways of im-proving the bath surface, and although a certain amount of surgery can be carried out with DIY products, for more serious cases it is advisable to call in experts who specialise in re-enamelling. This is the time to think about adding a stencil. Any painted surface is best applied before a glaze, especially on the inside of a bath. Failing this, the best way to make sure paints adhere to the surface is by preparing the vitreous enamel with hydrofloric acid. However, it is a complicated process, and before attempting it yourself you should contact paint specialists for advice.

PERIOD BATHROOM

This elegant bathroom has been given a thorough period treatment, from the authentic and reproduction fixtures and fittings down to Sally Walton's formal stencilling detail on the roll-top bath. The design is an enlarged version of the motif in the wallcovering and fabric, and has been painted using an ivory coloured artists' acrylic, highlighted with a second golden shade to add depth.

CHOOSING A STENCIL

BORDER OF BATHERS

The row of bathing huts, complete with energetic bathers in their striped suits, looks quite the part in this original bathroom with its giant shower head and roomy bath. In vivid emerald green, spiced with liquorice black, the border is a refreshing feature, and the chequered grid, stencilled onto both bath and tiles in ceramic paint, is the perfect accompaniment in this striking and spacious setting.

Once you have decided to stencil the bath, take time to choose a suitable design. If you are lucky enough to own a traditional, roll-top bath with claw feet, opt for a graceful stencil that echoes the curved sides. On the other hand, straight-sided baths, or bath panels, can take a more formal style: run a geometric border all around a hardboard panel, about 7 cm (3 in) from the edges, and it will give the impression of a moulding, and visually relieve the flush front. You should replace plastic bath panels with hardboard or wood as a base for stencilling. After stencilling, varnish your work to protect it from water. But do remember that bath panels need to be removable for plumbing access, so screw, rather than nail, your stencilled board into position. You will find that a broken painted finish looks particularly attractive as a base for stencilling: use white as a base and drag on top in the same shade as the bath; then decorate by dragging a complementary coloured paint across the stencil.

DECORATING TILES

If you prefer to sink back into the suds in more sumptuous surroundings, use stencils to help create a classy bathroom. Tiling from floor to ceiling with expensive tiles looks opulent, but can be costly. So, if the budget will not stretch that far, opt for cheap, plain, satin white tiles and stencil on a design of your choice with ceramic paint. If you are buying new, make sure the tiles are good quality, as some of the cheaper, imported ranges have imperfections in the glaze. To stencil on a tiled wall, first rub down the surface with coarse sandpaper, remove dust, and then prime with universal adhesive. Paint over with an undercoat, or any oil-based paint, and stencil with acrylic. Finally, seal the tiles with polyurethane to restore the gloss finish and protect them from water. As an alternative to a stencil-

led motif on each tile, you might like to stencil a large mural, in one colour, onto a section of the tiles. Try a stately pillar, with an urn, to give a Roman temple atmosphere; or a bright deckchair, bucket and spade for a seaside mood.

TILE CARE

The stencilled squares above and left were executed in ceramic paint, so cleaning of the tiles has to be carried out with care. Gentle wiping is recommended, avoiding rubbing or any abrasive cleansers. Matching the colours of acrylic and ceramic paint can be tricky, and several shades were mixed together to achieve the same green on both tiles and wall.

DISGUISING UGLY FEATURES

COTTAGE CLOAKROOM

A cottage cloakroom is made even cosier with stencilled borders in warm tan on a beige background. The tiled splashback is also stencilled, and a complementary stencilled fabric is made into a curtain, to conceal bathroom plumbing. Even the towels are stencilled in a co-ordinating design.

If pipes are much in evidence there is a good case for making a feature of them, rather than boxing-in. In modern settings, paint them a primary colour and stencil the larger ones with a simple shape. It is essential to use a tiny motif on pipes, as anything too big will disappear around the curve, and it is important to use plastic stencils, as card is too stiff to bend.

Stencils are a clever way of cheering up the essential, but rather ugly, frosted glass in bathroom windows. You will need to take care fixing the stencil in position, as if it is not firmly taped in place the bumpy surface makes it easy for the brush to slip under the stencil edge. Use glass paints and choose bold, sharp shapes – soft-edged florals will vanish into the texture of the pane. Flowers can work, but select some rounded art nouveau style tulips, or scatter three floating water-lilies, rather than use small be-ribboned posies.

CREATING A PERIOD LOOK

You might wish to decorate your bathroom in a traditional style by using an original design as the inspiration for a stencil. Look for Victorian or Art Nouveau tiles, trace off the design, and use one or more motifs on the walls.

If you have enough space, use a tiled washstand for storing toiletries and towels, and repeat the motif on plain fabric to hang at the window.

Polished wood looks superb in period bathrooms. Large old wardrobes are a source of good quality wood, and are often sold at reasonable prices at auction as their sheer bulk means they are not in demand. Use the wood to panel the bath in Edwardian fashion. First strip off any polish or varnish with a proprietary product, and then stencil either with wood dyes or a wood lightener, depending on the colour you require. Finish with several coats of polyurethane varnish.

Broom handles make good towel rails. Cut three or four to size and set them up one above the other, then decorate them with tiny stencils. In a traditional, Edwardian-style bathroom, stain the wooden handles mahogany, and then stencil in white along their length, or wind the stencil around on the diagonal to give a maypole effect.

CERAMIC PAINT ON A CISTERN

Pretty frilled curtains, reminiscent of blue and white china, have inspired stencilling on the sparkling white ceramic of the toilet cistern. The pattern is used sparingly so that the result is both fresh and unfussy. Stencilling with ceramic paint on this sort of surface is best tackled in one colour to avoid smudging the paint.

FLORAL MOTIF

Roses add a delicate touch to this traditional tiled bathroom. The bath has been coated with two coats of white, eggshell paint, sponged twice on top to soften the finish, and finally stencilled with signwriters' paints. Colleen Bery stresses the importance of using oil-based paint, rather than water-based emulsion, on cast iron – it inhibits rust.

ADDING HUMOUR

Wit works well in the the loo. It is the one room in the house that is viewed by all. Amuse visitors by stencilling a giant cow, or a group of lanky necked geese, on one of the walls. Make large stencils from several sheets of stencil card or film, and build up the picture in sections.

Use the same technique for stencilling a length of clear vinyl, and hang it up as a shower curtain. What about a drenched duck complete with holey umbrella, or a water pump, or a larger-than-life tap?

It is often a good idea to have reading matter in the bathroom. Make a montage of amusing or unusual news cuttings and surround it with a black and white stencilled border. (Use polyurethane as a protective coating.) You could even install a magazine rack and stencil pairs of spectacles onto the slats.

STENCILLED SHADES

Quite a spectacle! These stencilled motifs have been borrowed from a New York tee shirt and splashed all over the wall. The harlequin flooring and lipstick-red seat pull the whole room together, whilst the tee shirt that sparked off the idea in the first place is stretched over the window as a crazy screen.

DECORATING STORAGE AND ACCESSORIES

Everybody needs some sort of storage in a bathroom, and in a small area high-level shelves are often the only way of squeezing some in. Parallel pine slats make a good surface for piling up towels – and give more of an impression of space than would be achieved with solid shelving. Stencil on the underside to make them look prettier. This is best done before you put them up. You could then stencil the same design around a wall cabinet or mirror.

Bathrooms are the perfect place to house an interesting collection. However,

DECORATED CUPBOARDS

Clumps of rose-coloured sea pinks, stencilled within cupboard panels, look like a gallery of framed watercolour paintings in this airy bathroom. The aqua-washed walls and toning woodwork establish a freshness that provides the perfect canvas for the stencilling. To complete the picture, a rippling ribbon border edges the ceiling and a honeycomb framework, formed by strips of masking tape, graces the stripped floor.

paintings or photographs are not the best objects to decorate the walls with, as steam can seep behind the frames and ruin them. Instead, hang up some china plates, slipping in a stencilled plate among the group. Alternatively, you might fill a goldfish bowl full of pebbles, place it on the window sill, and then surround the window with a seashell border; or display decoy ducks on a shelf and scatter some stencilled ducks on the wall.

CO-ORDINATION

The motif used on the cupboards above has been repeated on the bath surround and low-level storage.

WINDOWS

Dressing a window is like choosing an outfit to wear. It is important to select the right style to complement the shape of the window, and to decide on a design that suits the mood of the room. Choose from shutters, blinds, ready-made or home-made curtains. Stencilling is an inexpensive way to create a co-ordinated 'designer' look. Further information on stencilling onto fabrics is given in the Soft Furnishings chapter (pages 84–6).

SIMPLE COMBINATION

It is not necessary to use an elaborate stencil to create an impact. This profusion of flowers, stencilled on shutters and wall, is built up from three single rose motifs, by Pavilion. The bonus of such a composition is that there is little planning involved – the blooms can be arranged by eye as the work progresses.

CHOOSING SUBJECTS TO STENCIL

To echo an oriental style, use a fabric at the window stencilled with bamboo, birds, blossom, fans or parasols. Choose a natural fibre with a texture, like a fine cotton slub weave, and fix it to a bamboo cane with tape ties.

If the room is filled with a pot pourri of objects from different eras, pick one dominant aspect and echo it in the stencil. Or mix moods by using two or more stencils. You will find that striped fabric is a good choice in an eclectic environment. Choose a printed stripe, or paint your own on a plain background, and run a stencil between the bands. This is a good trick for combining two elements, and is perfect for modern houses when the occupants have a passion for country prints.

In a kitchen try green garden herbs on a cream background to decorate a blind in an unstructured country room; or take the graphic shapes and steely colours of metal pots and pans as the inspiration for a blind in a room fitted with high gloss laminate units.

If you have an old, plain but functional venetian blind in the kitchen, you can stencil it using spray paint. Bear in mind that the design will only be visible when the blind is closed. However, the picture will turn into an abstract pattern, made up of many different colours, when it is open.

Roller blinds are perfect for stencilling, being flat, and having far less surface area than curtains. One bright, bold pattern will prove more effective than a bitty, detailed effect.

When choosing a stencil, bear in mind the fabric in the room and plan your use of stencilling accordingly. For example, to complement floral print curtains, you could pick out two or three flowers and stencil them onto a piece of painted wood, set up as a pelmet. Alternatively, if you have plain drapes 'in situ', simply add a

stencilled border along each edge.

Sheer fabrics at the window have a special, magical quality, especially when the light of a full moon or morning sun filters through them. Any stencilling on sheers should echo the effect, and must be both delicate and sparse, so that it doesn't interfere with the translucency.

FLORALS

Floral stencils needn't be traditional, nor a recognisable flower. Here, a stylised flower shape has been taken from the splashy print of the ruched blind, and used to frame the recessed window.

STARTING WITH THE WINDOW

'EMBROIDERED' BLIND

What appears to be exquisite embroidery and cutwork edging this roller blind is actually stencilling. The blind was made to leave ample fabric below the batten for painting. The design, derived from Indian handwork, was stencilled using fabric paints, and then edged with a 'broderie' pen and ironed on the reverse side to produce the raised effect. Some sections were cut away using a sharp scalpel.

Examine the window, and think of how it would look dressed in different ways. Study its shape, size, and form and its relationship to the rest of the room.

Large windows deserve a dramatic treatment, but the quantity of fabric needed makes most of us resort to skimping on the curtain width, or choosing a cheaper alternative. So instead, why not opt for generous amounts of plain fabric like sheeting, muslin or cotton duck, and make a feature of it by highlighting with a stencil.

Decide on the sort of drapery you want to use before selecting the stencil: put up a curtain pole and experiment with a length of white sheeting. Try swagging, tying and twisting, and letting the fabric cascade onto the floor. If it falls into loops over the

pole, it will work best co-ordinated with a classical looking stencil. Try a Roman style motif: stencil bold acanthus leaves on the fabric, or keep the drapes plain and stencil a pair of cherubs or scrolls around each top corner of the curtain pole, using rich colours such as saffron, crimson and bronze. However, if the drapes look better in a more formal arrangement, change the approach: exchange the sheeting for a heavier weight, plain-weave fabric, and stencil an all-over, brocade-like pattern, combining flowers with swirling scrolls. For a final opulent touch, finish off by trimming the edges with fringing and adding tassled tie-backs.

Small windows, on the other hand, often benefit from a simpler treatment. On a pretty, cottage window hang a pair of plain cotton curtains, just skimming the sill. Add a frilled pelmet in the same fabric, and stencil a meandering floral border along the edge. Outline the stencil in zig-zag stitch, on a sewing machine, and cut around the stitching, making sure all the raw edges are neatened so that they don't fray. Or for curtains that are purely decorative, and which aren't drawn, stencil one sprig of flowers on each curtain, make a chanelled heading and push a flat wooden batten through, gathering up the top. Attach the batten to the wall with square brackets. On curtains such as these, you should take care to select a stencil that is in keeping with the look – simple hedgerow flowers, such as poppies, speedwell or cow parsley, are far more suitable than roses or daffodils.

Whatever its size, surround a circular window with a basic stencilled border. And on slim windows that seem too small for curtains but still need privacy, make a beaded screen: stencil a miniature floral design onto satin ribbons, then thread the ribbons through glass beads, knotting at intervals to secure. Finish by framing the window with the same stencil.

If privacy is not a problem, you could set up plain or printed curtains as dress-drapes only, and decorate the pole. It is best to work on white painted poles, or on unfinished pine, so there is no varnish to remove. Entwine violas or daisies around the pole, and scatter larger versions of the same flower over the fabric. Or, add more colour by twisting together silk flowers and using them to hold the curtain back.

BUTTERFLY BLIND

Butterflies of all shapes and sizes, stencilled at random onto this roller blind, echo the design in the cream cotton lace draped over the pole. Some of the butterfly wings have been highlighted in a glittery fabric paint for extra shimmer. A lace motif has been cut from the fabric and appliquéd onto one cushion, whilst stencilled coral roses decorate another.

DRESSING WINDOWS WITHOUT FABRICS

WEDGWOOD SHUTTERS

These shutters are one of a set of five in a stately living room, and when all are closed and the curtains drawn, one wall of the room turns into a vast expanse of oyster silk. Stencilling provides visual relief from this monotonous uniform colour. The basket of flowers, in a Wedgwood blue shade of acrylic paint, is one of Paul Treadaway's earlier, more naive stencils, in which he utilises totally flat colour, with no shading.

Dressing a window need not necessarily mean using fabric. You can transform a plain, square window into an arched shape by painting a stencilled moulding at the top. Look at the architectural features around windows, both outside and inside municipal and historic buildings. You can stencil a carved stone look by sponging on paint, which gives the effect of a mottled surface (see pages 31 and 124).

Shutters make superb decorative features for impressive windows. Around small windows they give a French or Austrian flavour to a room. Reproduce this in a modest way by making your own small-

scale shutters from pine kitchen cabinet doors, and setting them into a frame. Stencil them with baskets of fruit or flowers, making sure you take off polish and varnish first with a proprietary remover. For a Scandinavian look, paint the shutters in white, and then stencil them with hearts and ribbons in a single colour.

Also, make the most of a recessed window by decorating the recess walls with stencils. Turn low, yet wide, sills into window seats and stencil a cushion cover to co-ordinate with the rest of the room (see page 92).

MARBLED URN SHUTTERS

This classic urn, again the work of Paul Treadaway, illustrates one of his favourite techniques – marbling through a stencil. The dusky pink acrylic paint was first applied with a brush, then taken off with a damp rag, to produce a mottled base, and the veins were added by using a feather. It is the uncontrolled direction of the feather which gives the characteristically uncontrived lines that mimic real marble.

DECORATING GLASS

If you long for a different style of window, change the shape just by using stencils. You can convert a plain pane into a latticed window by stencilling on criss-cross lines, and then dropping a tiny stencil into the centre of each diamond. Insects can look charming, especially the pretty flying ones, like ladybirds and bumble bees.

It is possible to alter the proportions of a large sheet of glass by sectioning-off some of it into smaller panes, using straight lines stencilled in black glass paint, and then stencilling a solitary flower inside each part. Similarly, if you love the solid, old, engraved glass windows, you can create the same impression on a plate window by stencilling only in white; paint a few small motifs (butterflies for example) onto a semi-circular fanlight window to achieve an etched glass look.

Stencilling on the glass of windows in a garden room is a fascinating way of linking indoors with the garden outside. Stick to flowers similar to those in the garden, and stencil them at a low level. You might introduce an element of fun by adding a cat's face peeping through the greenery. And, if you have double-glazed windows that open, try stencilling rows of flowers onto the inner of the two panes, so that one lies behind the other, and then 'planting' some fabric flowers into modelling clay between the layers of glass, to produce a profuse three-dimensional flowering effect.

SWANS ON GLASS
Elegant slender-necked swans, adapted by Gaby McCall from a photograph, make a magnificent stained glass panel out of a plain window. The stencil has been sprayed on the pane using auto paint. Note how all the bridges are made up of different curved lines, which enhance the shape of the birds and make each one unique – like birds with different markings.

DECORATING PELMETS, TRIMS AND TIE-BACKS

When you are faced with making the most of what you already have at the window, stencil some accessories to give it a lift. Stencilled tie-backs will help to offset some lifeless curtains. Make up some plain, lined ties in a contrasting fabric, and stencil them to tone in with the curtaining. Or combine plain and stencilled fabrics in a padded tie. Make the fabrics into tubes and fill them with polyester wadding. Then plait them together and join at each end.

You can use stencilling as a useful way of adapting old curtains to new windows by sewing on a stencilled band as an edging to add extra width or length.

Similarly, neaten a window with a stencilled pelmet. Exaggerate the stencilling shape by cutting the edge of the hardboard with a jigsaw so that it matches the outline of the stencil.

MIXING OLD AND NEW

Here, the stencil ties together a modern wallcovering and existing curtains, bridging the gap between old and new. The motif has been painted onto a pelmet, which fulfils the dual purpose of neatly concealing the curtain heading and disguising the different window levels.

SOFT FURNISHINGS

SOFA COVERINGS

Here, conservatory seating has been revamped to link it with the stencilled trellis theme in the adjoining kitchen (see page 44). The cane chairs were given a coat of white paint and new cushion covers were made up and stencilled. Linen union was chosen for the covering, as it is extremely tough and easy-to-care-for, and its tight weave easy to stencil. The broken lines within the striped design add visual interest, and maintain the light airy feel.

Stencilling is not restricted to the decoration of hard surfaces. With so many good quality fabric paints (see page 116) now available, all of which will withstand washing, there are a multitude of possibilities for stencilling soft furnishings around the home.

You can stencil on most types of fabric, although some are more responsive to fabric paint than others. Natural fibres like cotton are best because they absorb dye easily. Cotton/synthetic mixes, such as polyester/cotton, are fine too.

However, on fabrics that have a sheen or glaze, the paint tends to sit on the surface and give a semi-transparent finish. Consequently, you will often need to add further layers of paint to achieve a reasonable depth of colour. Fabrics that have a pile, like velvet or towelling, require a specific technique: the paint will need to be worked gradually into the pile, starting off by stippling on the colour, and then brushing it in with a circular motion.

PREPARING THE FABRIC

FABRIC TRIAL
This fabric design by Gaby McCall is a trial piece for a large wall hanging depicting an Indian tiger hunt. It illustrates how stencilling is often an interpretation rather than an exact replication of a subject. For example, an elephant on tiger hunt would never be highly decorated, but here the adornments add colour and interest; without them there would be an excess of grey. In addition, the bridges are incorporated into the design, and suggest muscular movement and folds of skin.

All new fabrics should be washed before stencilling so as to remove any size (the coating added to many new fabrics in order to maintain their crispness), otherwise, when applied, the fabric paint is likely to spread on the surface.

Stencilling on fabric is slightly more tricky than stencilling on walls, so it is advisable to start with small items, like cushion covers, and progress to more ambitious projects, like curtains, later on. There are several reasons for fabric being more difficult to work on: not only is there often a greater surface area to cover, especially with floor length curtains, there is also the problem that, usually, you work from top to bottom, and yet there are no registration marks on commercial stencils for lining them up vertically. It is not easy to ensure equal spacing of the stencil.

Measure the width of the fabric, allowing for turnings, and decide how many motifs you want to stencil across it. It is worth spending some time carefully marking out. This way you are far less likely to make mistakes, which is important as spills cannot be wiped off with a damp rag as they can from walls – any accidental daubs of paint will be soaked up into the fabric immediately.

CHOOSING COLOURS

It is worth looking at a few ranges of fabric paint before you select your colours, as the palettes vary considerably from manufacturer to manufacturer. Sometimes it is better to select a few pots close to the shade you want, and then to mix up your own. If you are combining different brands make sure they are compatible – that is, of the same base and curing process (air drying or heat setting).

Bear in mind the colour of the background you will be working on, and consider how strong an effect you will need. Remember that you won't produce the colour indicated on the pack unless the paint is on a white background. For example, if you are applying yellow paint to a blue fabric, the result may well be yellow, with a hint of green. The way around this is to first stencil the design in white, let it dry, and then repeat with the colour.

Also, the paint will transfer through the fabric, so lay several sheets of newspaper or thick card underneath to protect the surface that you are working on.

PAINTING CURTAINS

The crucial point to remember when stencilling fabric for curtains is to stencil a sufficient length to allow you to match the pattern when you are making up the curtain. In fact, it is far easier to cut the curtains and join the seams before you stencil. Just remember to start your design about 3.5 cm (1¼ in) from the selvedge, in order to allow for the turnings.

Handling a large quantity of fabric when stencilling can be tricky. So, make the work simpler by laying it out over a large table and a chair at either end. The paint dries so quickly there shouldn't be a problem of smudging when you move the fabric along, except in those instances when you need to use a lot of paint to establish the depth of colour – if, for example, you use a light colour on a pale background.

The easiest way to stencil an all-over design is to run the motif down, in columns. Start by leaving a space between every two columns that is wide enough to slip in an extra line if, at a later stage, you need to. Once you have stencilled these first columns, it is best to tack on some heading tape and temporarily hang the curtains to see how the patterns fall. With a standard pencil-pleat heading you will probably find that half of the lines will be hidden in the folds created by the gathers. The purpose of this exercise is to avoid having too many closely stencilled lines that will prove to have been a great deal of unnecessary work.

If you feel ambitious, play around with making up different patterns from one motif. Try dropping down every other column by half the size of the gap between the motifs, to make up a trellis shape. Or run the patterns across and down, in straight lines, to make up a grid. Remember that even if you are stencilling a random pattern, there should be a logical spacing between each motif to achieve a neat result.

OPULENT DRAPERY

The ultimate in glamorous bedrooms – a four poster bed lavishly swathed in the finest cloth. Although extravagant in quantity, the fabric is simple cotton muslin, stencilled with white lilies to emulate sheer lace. For projects such as this, where the stencilling is applied in the same colour as the background, it is essential to brush on the fabric paint heavily so that it is certain to show up.

DECORATING DUVET COVERS

AMERICAN FOOTBALL DUVET COVER

A stencilled duvet cover displays a young lad's first love – American football – and complements this splendid mural by Fred Wieland. Stencilled stars and stripes make an appropriate border to neaten the edge.

FILLING THE CENTRE

The star that forms a fundamental part of the design makes an appropriate central motif for this American football duvet cover.

People are always very sceptical about painting on bed linen because it needs such frequent washing, but, if properly applied and heat sealed, the fabric paint should stand up to as many washes as the duvet cover itself. It is important that you use a fabric paint as it will remain soft and pliable, whereas standard acrylic paints tend to stiffen and crack after a while. However, you could experiment with fabric felt pens or crayons to achieve a less-structured look.

Your main problem is likely to be tracking-down a plain cover to stencil. Most ready-made covers are embellished in some way. Often the best source of plain covers is from a mail order catalogue. Alternatively, you could stencil onto a good quality sheet, seam it with another, and add some Velcro to fasten the open end.

There is little point in stencilling standard flowers when there are so many florals to choose from in the stores. In order to make your design original try an exotic theme: stencil three jet black orchids, with jade stems, on a pale green cover; or a pride of golden lions on a dark blue background.

Finally, before you stencil your cover, slip a piece of cardboard between the layers to prevent the paint from seeping through to the reverse side.

. . . and pillowcases

It is simple to stencil the pillowcases to complement your duvet cover. If there are two, make an odd pair – perhaps one black sheep on a white pillow, facing one white sheep on a black pillow. For a more sophisticated look, stencil large scallop shells, in sugar-almond pink, onto the pillowcases, and team them with a collection of stencilled shells, in shades of ivory and duck egg blue, on the duvet cover. You should turn the painted side of the pillow over when in use, to protect the paint from abrasion, and extend its life.

STENCILLING BEDSPREADS

BEDSPREAD

Padding and stitching stencilled motifs can transform plain fabric into a sumptuous bedcover. In cool blue and a little yellow this quilt, by Ann Chiswell, looks particularly fresh and summery. The diamond-shaped quilting all over the cover ensures that the wadding is secured in place at regular intervals – as well as being decorative, this stops the filling moving during cleaning.

Traditionally, bedspreads, unlike duvet covers, tend to be heavy and, being protected by sheets, don't need frequent laundering. For this reason you can get away with using more luxurious fabrics, like silk, and combining stencilling with other techniques, such as quilting, appliqué and embroidery.

A combination of stencilling and quilting will give you a luxurious cover. It is a time-consuming task, so bear this in mind when you plan the design. Flowers are the obvious choice, but keep them large as small motifs will be too fiddly to pad. If you are tired of flowers, dot butterflies in blues and mauves, and finish the centres and wing details by hand or free-machine embroidery. Alternatively, spotty bows make a fun design, or you could stitch on small, ribbon bows (packets available from haberdashers) and stencil a painted replica between them.

Hand quilting in quantity will take months, so machining is advisable. Check that your sewing machine will take the thickness of wadding – you may need to hire an industrial model. First stencil your fabric, and then tack butter muslin to the back of the stencilled area. Cut out each shape from polyester wadding, using your stencil as a pattern. Slit the muslin at the back, push in the wadding, and restitch. Back the whole area with a large piece of fabric, or make an extra thick quilt by sandwiching a large piece of wadding between the two.

Mixing and matching plain quilting with flat stencils produces another interesting effect. Try quilting a star, made up from diamonds, in the centre of the cover and then scatter small, stencilled diamonds, in rainbow colours, around the edge.

If the idea of a patchwork quilt appeals, but time is a problem, create a traditional patchwork look by stencilling a geometric design. Use an authentic American quilt for your inspiration: look at museum collections of original work, and the many publications containing photographs and illustrations of the craft. You will find that patchwork quilts are readily translated into stencils because the balance of the shapes and the layout has already been worked out for you.

CUSHIONS

STENCILLED SILK CUSHIONS

These delicately painted cushions were designed and made by Ann Chiswell. Here, stencilling is combined with quilting, on silk, to produce varied relief. Ann cut the stencils from PVC fabric, which is both durable and flexible, and used fabric paints.

First attempts at fabric stencilling can easily be made up into cushions. Even if you feel shy about using strong colours elsewhere in the decor, cushions offer a small enough area to risk experimenting with. Try stencilling in jade green on a cream background and edging in navy, or decorate plain black with a touch of hot pink.

Use 'reverse' stencilling to create an

extremely effective co-ordinated look. Stencil a one-colour design onto the wall, then use the wall colour to stencil the same design onto cushions – try a blue motif on white walls then add some blue scatter cushions on the sofa, stencilled with the same design in white.

Frilled cushions contribute softness to a room. You can add a stencilled frill to ready-made plain cushions by measuring the distance around the cushion and cutting a strip of fabric about 12 cm (5 in) wide and one and a half times as long as the diameter of the cushions. Select a stencil, making sure that it is not too deep to fit on the frill.

Fold the fabric strip in half, press, then stencil a border design along the fabric, making sure that you leave at least 1.5 cm (½ in) plain at the edge to allow for a binding. Edge with bias and hand stitch to the cushion.

The prettiest cushions should be reserved for the bed. For the best effect, mix textures and trimmings – combine cream slub silk with satin and white lawn finished with lace and ribbons and stencilled to match. Machine ribbon in a criss-cross pattern and stencil a tiny flower in each diamond, or choose ivory lace as an edging and take a design from the motif.

FLOOR CUSHIONS

Stencilled cushions, large and small, piled on the floor in a teenager's room (see page 64) make an inexpensive seating arrangement.

TABLELINEN

TABLECLOTH AND TAPESTRY

Ruth Barclay's approach is unusual in both her choice of colour and fabric. Stencilled sweet peas in dark shades of damson make a refreshing change from the usual pastels. The stencilled window seat, by Saleena Khara, is also unusual in its imitation of a tapestry weave. The design was stencilled on unbleached calico, and parts of the motifs were edged with satin stitch.

A stencilled cloth can transform an ordinary table into something special. Perhaps the best way to show this type of cloth is to drape it over a side table, then top with objets d'art. You could make an extravagantly long cloth that trails on the floor, or a small stencilled cloth to layer over another. Cover the table with a basic plain cloth; stencil large flower heads along the edge of a smaller piece of sturdy fabric like a linen weave, outline with zig-zag machine stitching, then cut carefully around the shapes with sharp scissors.

On the other hand, tablecoverings that are meant to be functional need a totally different approach. First select a suitable fabric that can be easily laundered. Existing tablecloths are always a sensible start, but can be an expensive option. Instead look at furnishing fabrics; these are especially suitable because they are available in broad widths. Sheeting is a cheap alternative too, and usually has the added advantage of an easy-care finish. Although fabric paints are designed to withstand regular washing, it is advisable to restrict their use to areas that are not likely to get stained. If your tablecloth is meant for frequent use, restrict stencilling to the edges of the cloth.

MAKING FLOORCLOTHS

Stencilled floorcloths have a long history, dating back to the nineteenth century. They are made from canvas, which is painted and then varnished to make them hard wearing. Any canvas can be used – from natural cotton duck, available from artists' or theatre suppliers, to the green tarpaulin used for tents and boat covers.

First cut the canvas to size, allowing sufficient to turn over the edges (use a strong, contact adhesive to secure). Then apply a flat undercoat paint as a base – on coloured canvas you will need two or three coats. The canvas will wrinkle and slightly distort when the paint is wet. To eliminate this, when the paint is dry, roll up the canvas, secure with string, and leave it overnight. After the dry undercoated canvas has been straightened, measure out your design carefully, using the same procedure as for centering stencilling on ceilings (see page 53).

CLASSIC FLOORCLOTH
Stencilled floorcloths, popular in the late nineteenth century, are now in vogue again. This one was made from a piece of boat tarpaulin, painted in white emulsion (latex) paint, stencilled and sealed with polyurethane.

FURNITURE

Any furniture can be stencilled successfully, provided the surface is prepared correctly. It is essential to remove any dirt, polish, wax, varnish, or unsound paint before you start. And a shellac knotting compound must be applied to any knots in the wood, to prevent resin staining or blistering the finished decoration.

FLORAL CABINET

An elderly piece of furniture can often be improved with tasteful stencilling. The beauty of this aged cabinet has certainly been enhanced by stencilling elegant irises on the doors.

STENCILLING TABLES AND CHAIRS

Before you stencil a table it is worth considering what you are going to put on it. For example, the stencil on a dining table should complement the crockery that you usually use with it. It should not overpower it – with floral china especially, borders and motifs should be kept to a minimum. Similarly, the decoration on a dressing, or occasional, table should both reflect and complement the knick-knacks on display.

Obviously you can stencil any chair in any room in the house. However, stencilled chairs in the kitchen really can brighten up the whole room. First paint them a cheerful colour, and then run a motif along the back, front and seat. Again, take care to choose a stencil that is in keeping with the decor, and in proportion to the chair.

ELEGANT BENCH

This slender bench may at first sight seem too narrow for painted decoration, but the elegant lines of the spindles and frets are well suited to miniature stencils. A reduced version of a commercial border – field flowers in faded shades of rose and willow – complements the upholstered tapestry seat.

STENCIL DETAIL

Intricate detail stencilling like this is best tackled using a small brush (size 1 or 2). In an area exposed to constant wear stencils should be varnished for protection.

DECORATING STORAGE FURNITURE

PEDESTAL DESK

*This desk, by Robert and
Colleen Bery, is sponged with
eggshell paint, then decorated
with stencilled bows. Note how
the motifs are attractively
placed, with the ribbon tails
trickling down over the drawers.*

The easiest way to tackle a chest of drawers
is to scatter a motif over the drawer fronts,
changing the positioning of the stencil
according to where the handles fall. A tiny
stencil on wooden pulls can be very
effective, and a fun idea for children is to
stencil a little fairy on one of the feet, or
emerging from one of the drawers. A
border surrounding the drawers can look
pretty, but needs careful planning – you
have to keep the stencil in proportion to the

size of the chest, and you should pay
particular attention to corners: mitred ones
look neat on a chest.

Old, wooden blanket chests are superb
items of furniture for stencilling, and the
dome-topped kind look especially attractive. As you are dealing with a large
expanse of wood, there is no need to
confine yourself to borders and trims. You
can work out a pattern to cover the entire
lid, or the whole piece of furniture. Large,

WATER LILY SIDEBOARD
A sophisticated, birch sideboard was stippled in steely blue-grey, lined in sharp lemon, and then stencilled, by Colleen Bery, with water lilies and humming birds, using signwriters' paints and decorators' paintbrushes.

old wardrobes can be embellished successfully with garlands of flowers, but use fine, delicate flowers for smaller items. You can integrate them into the room by running a border along the top edge, front and sides, and continuing it around the walls at the same height.

A large expanse of white doors on built-in cupboards can be broken-up with a geometric border, or a series of small floral motifs. This approach is particularly effec-tive if you first apply one of the special paint techniques (see page 124) as a background to your stencilling.

Exactly the same principle applies to your old kitchen units: a paint technique background and a stencilled motif can update the entire kitchen. Even melamine faced units can be given this treatment. Key them first by rubbing down with wet and dry paper, and then cover with several coats of eggshell finish paint.

DECORATING CHILDREN'S FURNITURE

DECORATED DESK
Stencilled motifs give new life to a solid oak school desk. The wood was stripped back, sanded down and, with no primer or undercoat, white emulsion (latex) was rubbed into the wood in the direction of the grain. The paint was wiped off in places to establish two tones of colour. Gaby McCall distressed the finish to give it an aged appearance.

The first, and most important point to remember when painting and decorating furniture for children's use, is that any paint used must be non-toxic. So, specifically choose a special nursery paint. As the paint will be oil-based, and therefore slow drying, you should stick to a simple design, and maybe just one colour. Otherwise the job will take a very long time, as you will have to wait for about 48 hours, depending on temperature and humidity, for each colour to dry before repositioning the stencil. An alternative method is to use a polyurethane spray paint. As for ideas, well, an illustrated book of nursery rhymes will provide both the inspiration and the designs.

WORKING ON BARE WOOD

If you intend to stencil on bare wood, there are a number of options open to you: the warm, rich tones of mahogany, pine or oak allow you to use earthy colours, such as reds, browns and gold. Try wood dyes, as well as paints – they produce very interesting effects. Broadly speaking, if you stick to the colours found in natural woodland you won't go far wrong.

On the other hand, stencilling onto a bleached-out, limed wood grain is very much in vogue (see page 121). You should be careful that any decoration on this surface is in sympathy with the paleness of the wood – that is, of simple outline, uncomplicated and that all colours are soft, muted and washed out. Stencil crayons give a particularly soft effect.

TRADITIONAL TOY CHEST

The rocking horse, drum, moon and star motifs were chosen for their charming Victorian style. The chest was antiqued with a finishing coat of polyurethane tinted with a dash of rust coloured paint.

STENCILLING ON PAINTED SURFACES

FIRESCREEN
Paul Treadaway started by painting the board, and then spraying in black, from the base upwards, to establish a sense of depth. A mottled urn formed the centrepiece, and the greenery was stencilled by overlapping just one fern motif, using various shades of green.

CLASSIC MIRROR
A rope border spray stencilled onto the frame adds a classic touch to this otherwise plain hall mirror.

GRAND PIANO
An unlikely site for a stencil, but certainly one way of adding a cheerful note to a plain piano.

Again, there are a number of options open to you if you wish to stencil onto painted furniture. You can work on a traditionally painted surface, that is, one that has been primed, undercoated and finished with two coats of eggshell topcoat. Alternatively, you can use a special paint technique as a background to your decoration (see page 124). Whichever method you employ, you will find that pale shades are more subtle and sophisticated than brighter colours.

A dragged background (see page 124) will give the appearance of a two-tone, woven fabric, or of raw silk. It is a good idea to start with a fairly small project, such as dragging a coffee table to blend in with the surrounding decor. You should use a complementary, muted colour when you apply the stencil. However, if you are decorating a chest of drawers in a child's bedroom, you could use vibrant colours for the dragging, such as red on white or green on yellow, and then add a stencilled border of small soldiers, or small motifs on the drawer knobs. When you have mastered the technique you can progress to more adventurous projects, like updating kitchen cabinets. Choose a stencilled motif to suit the shape of the doors and the character of the kitchen – a bunch of dried

flowers or herbs, or a basket of fruit, would suit a country kitchen for example.

Sponging on a background (see page 124) produces a softer looking finish than dragging. It looks like rough stone or a cloudy effect, depending on how you apply the paint. If you have some stark white cupboards in a neutral-coloured sitting room, sponge them beige on cream and stencil a coffee-coloured border around the edge. Equally, you might have a smart 'high-tech' study that is spoilt by an out-of-keeping old wooden chair. Just prepare the wood, sponge it in grey, and stencil a stylish, geometric motif across the back.

Rag rolling will give you a random, sparse colour effect that looks like lightly crumpled fabric (see page 124). The delicate finish is particularly suitable for use with pastel colours in bedrooms. You should select a fairly bold design and reasonably strong colours when stencilling on this finish – soft, pastel flowers can disappear into the texture. Rag rolling a dressing table, and then stencilling can be very effective.

If your bedroom has rag rolled walls, topped with a stencilled border, you should continue the effect along fitted cupboard doors as the uninterrupted motif will make the room look larger.

WICKER CHAIR

Most families have a Lloyd Loom chair like this hidden away somewhere. This example has been given a new lease of life by spraying it with white paint, and then stencilling flowers on top.

SMALL OBJECTS AND ACCESSORIES

Stencilling allows you to add individuality to many of the small objects that you have around the home. At the same time, it makes it possible to integrate these accessories into the surrounding decor.

A FRIVOLOUS NOTE

Clefs and notes make a graphic stencil on this cloth and wooden tray, and nicely complement the coffee set. The tray required several coats of polyurethane varnish for protection, although this does yellow the paint slightly.

PAINTING MIRRORS AND PICTURE FRAMES

COUNTRY MIRROR

The simple rose, designed by Melanie Stock, rambling around the frame and set against pine tongue and groove, evokes a definite country mood. The soft coral colour is as much a contributory factor to the style as is the stencil design.

Mirror and picture frames present few problems, and are amongst the easiest of objects to stencil. If the frames are wood, the preparation required is the same as that for furniture, and you will find that choosing one of the various special paint techniques (see page 124) will provide you with a very effective background for stencilling your motif onto.

The relatively small surface area of a frame means that you will have to use a tiny stencil. Most commercial stencils, being designed primarily for wall decoration, are too large. However, some miniatures are available, or you can always design and cut your own.

It is possible to stencil onto glass, and you should use either stained glass paints, which give a charming, translucent finish, or auto spray paints, which should be sprayed on lightly, until the glass begins to lose its transparency. For the best effect you should select colours that are not too dense. For example, opt for charcoal grey rather than black, so that the finish does not appear too solid (see page 82).

DECORATING BASKETS AND BOXES

PICNIC STENCILS

The large, bow-wrapped wicker hamper in the background was stencilled in a similar way to the blind on page 66, but in reverse – the bow shape was outlined with masking tape and then sprayed with auto paint. The pretty yet practical picnic plate was stencilled, then transferred by a technical process which is unsuitable for D.I.Y., but can be carried out by an Australian company with a U.K. base, who offer a mail order service (see page 128).

BOXES FOR ALL PURPOSES

Three wooden containers have been given a lacquer look by painting in acrylic, stencilling and finishing off with five coats of polyurethane varnish. The stencilling style captures the charm of traditional gold leaf painting typically found on cast iron sewing machines.

Wicker-work looks very attractive when stencilled with spray paints. However, it is important to choose a bold design, as any patterns with intricate details will be hidden in the basket weave. You can achieve exciting results by making a pattern from masking tape and spraying over it to get a negative stencil effect (see page 66).

You will have to use the white, Chinese-type wicker, as the heavy, English willow is too dark, and the weave too coarse and uneven, to take a stencil.

Whether you have tiny boxes for hiding away paper clips, screws and nails, or larger boxes for sorting out sewing accessories, or even larger ones for storing shoes and hats, stencilling them will brighten them up, integrate them into the decor of a particular room, and indicate the contents.

Make use of ordinary household containers, such as sturdy chocolate and cosmetic boxes. Paint out any brand names with a couple of coats of paint. You could even use a paint technique (see page 124) as a background for your stencilling. Cut your own stencils to depict the shape of the contents, or, if the box will be on show, pick up a motif from the room.

STENCILLED BOXES

Two sturdy wooden boxes, appropriately stencilled with wet weather footwear, provide fun storage. Gaby McCall rubbed eggshell paint into the bare wood, ragged a second shade on top, to get a mottled effect, and then stencilled with auto sprays. Note the elegant, stylised lettering – chunky conventional stencilled letters would have been too heavy for the delicate colouring.

BORDERING FAVOURITE COLLECTIONS

A few pictures thoughtfully grouped together can be linked with a stencil, either by surrounding the arrangement with a border or by adding a single motif at each corner. However, take care to opt for a stencil that will embellish the gallery, without overpowering the subjects. It must be of a suitable style, scale and colour to complement the pictures. Stencil crayons are particularly suitable for this as the tones are always muted.

A few companies make stencils for do-it-yourself 'framing' of arrangements. These are reproductions of the kind originally used in the eighteenth century around unframed prints, but can be used to the same effect around contemporary framed pictures and other objects. The commercial varieties include bows, bells, swags and tassels often made up into intricate chains, ropes and ribbons.

PICTURE DISPLAYS

In this display of objects on a wall the layout of the various items is as important to the overall appearance as the actual items themselves. Stencilling is used to make a feature of the arrangement, and imitate the traditional eighteenth century fashion for 'framing' prints.

WALL COLLECTION

Collections are meant to be shown off. Here, a crayoned border surrounds a group of hearts made from an interesting mix of materials – wood, straw and terracotta juxtaposed with dried lavender and wax. A pencil guideline is essential for stencilling the oval shape, which in this case was drawn using an oval meat plate as a template. If the collection grows, the border can be painted over and stencilled again.

DECORATING CERAMICS, GLASS AND TINWARE

STENCILLED CERAMICS

It is a shame to fill this cheerful bowl with anything but water. It makes an intriguing table centre and finger bowl at dinner parties, especially with a few flower heads or floating candles drifting on the surface. The jolly frogs are taken from a book on Chinese ink painting, and have been stencilled onto glazed white ceramic with two coats of 'on-glaze'. The bowl was then re-fired at 720°C (1328°F).

Probably the most difficult area, when it comes to decorative paintwork, is that of applying paint to a glazed ceramic surface. Stencilling is the perfect way of putting a pattern onto plain china, but finding a paint with 'staying power' can prove difficult.

To be blunt, there are few media that are entirely suitable for stencilling onto crockery, that will withstand everyday use and washing. Most ceramic paints available on the market are fine for decorative objects, like the vases illustrated on page 109, but they will scratch off fairly easily when washed – you would need to take care even with the relatively infrequent cleaning these require.

You could turn this impermanence to your advantage: that is, by stencilling some glazed ceramics with a particular design, and in various colours, and then, after a period of time, easily removing your work, with some water and a scourer, and redecorating with a new stencil and colours.

There are only two ways around this problem, and both have drawbacks: firstly, you can use 'on-glaze', a specially formulated medium which needs to be fired at 720°C (1328°F). Stencil one coat, leave to dry, then stencil a second coat. Too little paint can result in a faded image. It is possible to hire some time in a kiln to refire the article(s). Some schools, colleges and ceramic specialists offer the service. Unfortunately, it is not unknown for cracking to occur during this process. The risk of this can be minimised by selecting good-quality china as a base. Secondly, you can restrict your stencilling of tableware to totally functional melamine plates. You cannot carry out this process directly yourself – an Austalian company, operating worldwide and using a special technique, transfer your design from paper onto the dishwasher-proof malamine plates (see page 104). Whilst the reproduction of your work is excellent, you are restricted to drawing

PASTEL POTS

These attractive vases show that glazed ceramic is a rewarding surface to stencil. Unfortunately the finish is easily damaged, and thus requires great care when dusting and washing. However, this does mean that when you tire of the design you can scrape it off and redecorate.

your pattern with water-based felt pens, which give a bright, child-like finish.

Before decorating tinware, the surface should be prepared by removing any rust, treating with a rust inhibitor, and then coated with a metal primer. Spray paints will provide good coverage, and enamel paints are excellent but slow drying. The most typical old tinware decoration was of basic, rustic shapes, and your stencilling will be most effective if you echo this simple look.

It is vital to prepare the surface of glass well before stencilling. It must be spotless and thoroughly dry or the paint will not adhere. So, wipe over with methylated spirits. Stencilling with matte or eggshell varnish has an unusual effect that, when dry, resembles frosted glass. Any plain glass items can be given this treatment. For a coloured design, add a drop of oil-based paint to the varnish (one part colour to fifteen parts varnish).

GLASS SHADE

Julia Roberts cut this charming floral stencil specifically to fit this light, and applied it with auto spray paint. Note how the solitary bud positioned between the full bloomed flowers balances the design.

CREATING INDIVIDUAL STATIONERY

DECORATIVE PAPER

Stencilling wrapping paper is far more fun than buying the commercial variety. Here, three pre-cut stencils, were applied to large sheets of drawing paper (though rolls of lining paper will do). The soft colouring was achieved by using stencil crayons. Coloured luggage labels make original gift tags.

Stencilling will transform ordinary note-paper into classy, personalised stationery. Try cutting a stencil (see page 115) of your own monogram or family crest. This is quite easy to do.

To achieve a sophisticated look, stencil in the same colour as the background paper, but deepen the tone slightly so that it shows up. Poster or fabric paints, craft acrylics and stencil crayons are ideal for this. Metallic paints produce a chic, spark-ling effect when stencilled in gold onto a

cream background, or silver onto a black one. As they tend to be very liquid, use an extra dry brush.

Also, it is easy to churn out unique and inexpensive wrapping paper with a stencil. Use something cheap and tough as your base – lining paper is ideal – and scatter geometric shapes over it, in assorted col-ours, for a birthday theme, employ the same design in red and green for Christ-mas, and just a add a touch of glitter for a wedding or anniversary.

MAKING STENCILLED CLOCKS

There are no limits to the form or shape a stencilled clock can take. Ours (left) was made from an old kitchen cabinet door, and stencilled with country garden flowers, to evoke a Tyrolean style.

To make any clock, drill a hole in a piece of suitable material (this could be anything from a sheet of board to a ceramic plate). Paint in a background colour, and then add the stencilled decoration, picking up a motif from the room in which the clock will stand or hang. Finally, attach a quartz mechanism to the back.

CRAFTED CLOCK

This traditional looking painted clock started out as a kitchen cabinet door. It was reshaped and sanded down before stencilling, with ragged petalled flowers and ribbons, gave it a new lease of life.

DESK ACCESSORIES

Stencil crayons can produce subtle, blended colours and can be used on a variety of different surfaces. Stencilled motifs in gentle hues of silver, peach and cream turn basic writing paper into exclusive stationery, and a simple chipboard box into an elegant planter. Smaller, hand-cut stencils decorate the lamp and picture frame to make a co-ordinating set.

TECHNIQUES AND MATERIALS

As with any practical craft, it is important to study the instructions before you embark on any stencilling project, not only to learn about the different materials available and the basic steps to follow, but to understand the pitfalls you might come across and to pick up any tips that may be applicable to a specific method. Although there are certain guidelines in this section that you need to digest, you shouldn't worry about making mistakes – there is far less chance of making an error in stencilling than most other handicrafts.

The recommendations in the following pages are aimed at helping you to perfect technique, it is up to you as an individual to experiment with different approaches and media. Every professional stenciller has his or her own tried and tested method. It is, however, always wise to start with a commercial stencil, at least until you get the 'feel' of the art, and the clear plastic type are certainly easier for beginners to handle.

COMMERCIAL STENCILS

Most manufactured stencils come pre-cut in a wide range of sizes and designs.

Nowadays, most commercial stencils are made from Mylar®, a clear plastic material that is easy to clean, flexible, very strong and much simpler to use than the traditional waxed-board type. The most basic designs require just one sheet, whereas more complex patterns may need up to four or more separate sheets for the application of different colours. You won't have a problem with lining up the stencil each time you change colour, because printed marks on the stencil sheets allow for easy registration.

The flexibility of Mylar® means it can be bent easily into corners, or wrapped around a curved surface, and its transparency allows you to see what has been painted already, and to keep working in a continuous line.

Waxed card stencils are best used with spray paints, because water-based paint tends to make the card soggy, so it stretches and distorts. In contrast, aerosol paints harden and strengthen the card as each layer of colour is applied. Card stencils tend to be fragile, and do not last long if subjected to constant use. They are not easy to clean, and paint will gradually accumulate along the cut edges, thus slowly decreasing the size of the design.

MAKING YOUR OWN STENCIL

You can cut a stencil from virtually anything, but you should consider its intended use before deciding which material to cut it from. Strong paper or card is fine for small areas of stencilling and basic shapes. However, larger stencils, requiring greater detail, are best cut from purpose-made materials:

Stencil paper

This is a semi-transparent, waxed paper that allows the stencil to be cut directly from a design placed underneath it. The paper does not stand up to extensive use.

Stencil card

Flexible, oiled stencil card is more durable than stencil paper. However, it is not transparent, so designs must either be drawn directly onto it, before cutting, or transferred onto it from paper, via carbon. If acrylic paints (see page 116) are used on card, a stippling action is essential to avoid tearing.

Transparent plastic

Although generally referred to as acetate, the clear plastic most often used for stencilling is actually made from polyester, and known as Mylar®. The frosted kind of Mylar® (single matte) is preferable, as it is easy to draw onto the matte surface. Its shiny reverse is suitable for painting through, and makes cleaning easier. Also, the matte surface tends to grip without slipping. This makes it possible for a number of sheets to be superimposed for colour separations, rendering masking unnecessary.

Mylar® is sold in different thicknesses, referred to as 'thou' or microns. Four thou (.004/100 micron) is the ideal one to use, being flexible yet strong. Five thou (.005/125 micron) is thicker and tougher, and so more difficult to cut. Three thou (.003/75 micron), tends to be too bendy and thin.

DRAWING THE DESIGN

Virtually any illustration or photograph can be converted to a stencil. You could trace directly onto transparent, plastic stencilling material, but this would be expensive if you made mistakes. Therefore, it is a good idea to trace from your picture onto tracing paper first.

To enlarge or reduce the size of a design, overlay a sheet of tracing paper, marked with a grid, trace the design, and then copy the motif, square by square, onto a smaller or larger grid. Finally, transfer your design from tracing paper to clear stencil material

Note: *Stencil paper is best for projects where the stencil will only be used a few times, such as stencilling on roller blinds or furniture.*

Note: *The paler variety of stencil card is easier to draw on than the usual darker tan type.*

Note: *Make sure that your fingers are away from the path of the knife in case of accidents.*

STENCILLING TECHNIQUE

1 *Working on a flat non-slip surface, with your free hand firmly on the pre-marked stencil, cut with a sharp knife.*

2 *Position the cut stencil on the surface to be decorated, and fix with low-tack masking tape.*

Note: *Stencils can be painted in a number of ways, as shown on page 119.*

3 *Pour a little paint onto a saucer, then dip in the brush tip. Dab off excess on absorbent paper.*

4 *Hold the brush upright and dab on the paint with an up-and-down motion.*

by tracing again.

An alternative method is to 'print' your design directly onto Mylar®, by hand-feeding the sheet of A3 or A4 material through a photocopier, matte side up, with the design, as usual, face down on top of the machine.

Stencils with and without bridges

When you are drawing a stencil of a flower, for example, at the point where one section joins another, such as where the leaves meet the stem, you must separate them with a bridge. This is a solid piece, about 3 mm (⅛ in) long, left in the material to ensure rigidity. If an opening in the stencil is too long, and isn't bridged at any point, the stencil may move as you are using it, and your brush can then slip underneath. Bridges also give the design a typical stencil look, and provide a convenient surface on which to attach masking tape when you wish to protect certain sections of the pattern when applying a particular colour.

However, on the occasions when you intend to use more than two colours, or you want a hand-painted look, you can draw a stencil without using bridges. This means the design will need to be divided into sections according to colours – each colour being allocated its own stencil sheet. Where two colours meet, allow an overlap of about 3 mm (⅛ in), to avoid any gaps in the finished work. You should not use this method when stencilling long, wavy outlines or intricate designs, as the sheet may warp when painted if there are no bridges to strengthen it.

REGISTRATION

Any design that is to be repeated will need registration marks to help with positioning it, and to ensure it is kept straight. Copy your design onto tracing paper. Decide how many colours you wish to use, and take the same number of pieces of stencil card. The card should be large enough to allow at least a 2.5 cm (1 in) margin around the design. Cut the tracing paper and stencil cards to the same size. Tape the tracing paper and stencil card together, one above the other, and cut a shaped notch through all the layers, in two opposite corners, top and bottom. Matching up the notches, place carbon paper between your traced design and the first stencil card, and trace all the parts that belong to stencil number one. Make sure you mark the stencil card with a number and colour. Repeat this process for each colour.

When two or more sheets of Mylar® are used in a stencil, lining up is easy because of the transparency. Using a felt tip pen and broken lines, mark on the second sheet parts of the design that feature in the first sheet.

After the stencils have been cut out, tape stencil number one onto the surface to be painted. Draw around both notches onto the surface, using a pencil. Apply the first colour, and when the stencil is dry, replace it with the next stencil, and line up the notches with the pencil marks. This way you can be sure that the stencil is correctly positioned. The second colour can be applied and subsequent colours, until the stencil is completed.

Similarly, if you are using your design as a repeated border, punch a hole in the same position, through both the right and left hand sides. Make a pencil mark through the holes and onto the surface you are working on, to ensure the different sections can be placed in the same position when you are applying each colour.

CUTTING A STENCIL

To make a stencil draw or trace your design onto card or Mylar® and cut it out with a sharp scalpel or craft knife. Special cutting boards are available, or you could use a flush surface, like laminated board or bevelled-edged glass.

To cut a stencil from Mylar®, put the stencil design on a flat, non-slip surface and place the stencil material on top of it. Tape the stencil material to the design, and the design to the board. Make sure you leave at least a 2.5 cm (1 in) margin all around so that later on any overbrushed paint goes onto the card, and not onto the surface you are stencilling. Use a scalpel or craft knife to cut out the stencil, making sure the blade is sharp.

Firmly place your free hand on the stencil, with your fingers pointing away from the path of the knife, in case of accidents. Cut towards you, and along the drawn line, with the knife almost perpendicular, that is, slightly leaning away from the design.

When dealing with a complex design, begin by cutting out the smaller shapes, as removing the larger areas first will weaken the stencil for the subsequent cutting. When you need to turn a corner, move the stencil around the position of the blade, rather than moving the blade around the curves of the stencil.

When cutting out a stencil from card, the procedure is the same, except that the outline of the design will be on the surface, rather than showing through from below.

Note: The best cutting boards are made from a self-healing, rubberised material and have a printed grid that assists with accurate positioning of the stencil.

*Note: A blunt blade is **more** dangerous than a sharp one, as you are likely to place more pressure on the knife and therefore slip.*

Note: Don't worry if your cutting is uneven, as ragged edges often add to the charm and individuality of a hand-crafted look. If they do bother you simply re-trim.

PAINTS AND DYES

There are various products available that are suitable for stencilling. Which you choose to use will depend on their different properties and your requirements.

Acrylics

There are acrylic-based paints specially formulated for stencilling. They are fast-drying and easy to remove from brushes and stencils. Artists' acrylics are a good substitute, but take longer to dry. Both types can be diluted with water to give quite subtle effects, and both can be used on fabrics, but the fabric should not be washed or dry cleaned after use.

Fabric paints

The paints designed specially for fabrics are usually water-based, yet can be laundered. Most are 'set' by pressing with a hot iron on both sides of the fabric, once the paint has dried; a few are air-drying. Heat-expanding textured paint in a tube is suitable for most fabrics. Apply directly from the tube nozzle for outlining.

Emulsion (latex) paint

Emulsion paint can be used on most surfaces, but because it has such a high water content, you need to take more care to keep a dry brush during application. There is a vast range of colours available, although apart from trial pots the minimum quantity you can buy is 0.5 litre.

Oil-based paints

Oils can be used in situations either where water resistance is an important factor, or for achieving a shiny surface on top of a gloss base. Usually, they are slow-drying, so are only suitable for minimal application, such as on furniture, where there is little repetition of motifs, and the stencil doesn't need to be lifted and replaced, thereby risking smudging. To remove oil-based paints from the surface of the stencil you will need to use white (mineral) spirit.

Japan paint

This fast-drying, oil-based paint is ideal for use on any surface from wood to metal, glass, ceramics and plastics. However, being of a very thin consistency, it is best to apply it using the 'dry brush method'.

Universal paints

Some speciality craft paints and stains are especially formulated for use on a variety of materials (wood, ceramics, glass, plastics, metals and fabrics).

Ceramic paints

There are basically two types of paints for use on ceramics: some that are applied cold to glazed ceramic (strictly decorative, they scratch off during wear); others, known as 'on-glaze', need to be fired in. On-glaze must be put on heavily as it fades during firing.

Stencil crayons

Stencil crayons and paint sticks are suitable for most surfaces. They are a solid form of oil-based paint and produce a soft colour.

Spray paints

Sprays give a sheen finish, and can be applied to most surfaces, including metal. The sprays are fast drying, but need to be used with care, as it is easy to overspray, and end up with too much colour.

Consequently, they should be sprayed on in short, sharp bursts, and the colour built up gradually, in layers. You will find the sprays useful in situations where brushing is difficult, such as on uneven surfaces like wicker-work. However, because they tend to spread during application, masking the surrounding areas is necessary.

Use a guard to control the amount of spray – cut a small piece of card about 30 × 10 cm (12 × 4 in), crease it down the middle and use it as a barrier when you just need a smattering of colour.

Always have a clean-up kit of acetone and cotton buds (Q-tips) available to wipe off any stray spray.

If a can becomes clogged after constant use, clear the nozzle with a pin and then wipe it with acetone.

Note: Because spray paints give off fumes, you must work in a well-ventilated room.

Note: Poster and water colours, felt pens and crayons aren't suitable for stencilling on walls, floors or furniture. However, children can use them with stencils for decorating paper and card.

Note: If you require a soft look, in keeping with the room, stencilling with oil crayons will be particularly effective.

Signwriters' paints

These multi-purpose paints are fairly thick in consistency. They are suitable for any surface, especially floors, as they give good coverage, however, the colour range is limited.

Wood dyes

Dyes and stains for wood tend to be runny, but have a pretty, opaque effect that allows grain to show through. A very dry brush should be used, and any excess dye wiped onto a cloth before starting.

STENCILLING A CHEST

1 First prepare the surface by removing any varnish or polish and sanding until smooth.

2 Work out the best arrangement of each stencil before launching into the project.

3 Finish off by varnishing to preserve the stencilling. Use a proprietary antique varnish, or mix a little coloured stain with a standard varnish.

TOOLS

Unless you are spraying, you will require a brush to apply paint through the stencil. The traditional stencil brush is short, with a stubby handle, and has very stiff bristles, all of the same length. However, this sort of brush is difficult to work with, as the bristles don't absorb much paint – it just sits on the tips, which makes it easy to apply too much colour. So, it is important to use a brush that is soft enough to avoid this problem, and also which will allow you to make easy, circular motions to achieve a smooth finish. Choose one which has bristles that will spread a little when pressed against a hard, flat surface. Some companies make domed-topped stencil brushes and a few experts who use a stippling method favour these – the shaped bristles make it easier to get into the edges of the stencil and achieve shading without pressing hard.

Extra large brushes are available for floors, although some stencillers prefer to use standard decorators' brushes. Special fabric stencil brushes are available with cotton bound bristles.

You will find small containers are useful for mixing paints in. Use an old saucer or a ceramic tile for small amounts, but for large quantities use small bowls, take-away trays or cartons. Finally, a platform-ladder and/or a sturdy workbench are useful, especially when you are working on ceilings.

PUTTING ON THE COLOUR

Position the stencil on the surface to be decorated, and fix it in position by using low-tack masking tape, or adhesive spray mount. Pour a small amount of paint into a saucer, starting with the lightest colour that you will be using. Dip the tip of your brush in the paint, and dab off any excess onto absorbent paper or lint-free cloth.

It is important to select the right size of brush for the job. Generally, sizes 2 and 4 are best for small designs, such as on boxes or ceramics, but for walls and floors you should use bigger brushes. Hold the brush upright, and dab on the paint using an up and down motion. If you are using crayons, it is a good idea to use the uncut area of the stencil as your palette. Then you can pick up the paint from its surface, onto the tip of the brush, and work it into the design, moving from the outside into the centre. When you have filled all the sections, carefully remove the stencil.

When using oil-based, crayon-type paint, you will find that it will accumulate around the edge of the stencil more than an acrylic paint would do. So you will need to clean the stencil more regularly with white (mineral) spirit, or turpentine, to ensure a crisp edge to your work.

If you find that the bridges begin to rise when stencilling, pin them down by pressing with the scalpel tip or the point of a pencil. And remember to check, from time to time, that the back of the stencil is clean.

Using more than one colour

The easiest way to apply more than one colour is to have a different stencil sheet for each one. Many commercial stencils come with several sheets, thereby making colour separations straightforward, and they are pre-printed with clear registration marks, so lining up is simple, and it is difficult to make any mistakes.

However, if you are using a commercial stencil that only has one sheet, you will have to mask off the sections not needed for the first colour. Use small pieces of low-tack masking tape.

STENCILLING ON DIFFERENT SURFACES

Before starting in earnest, you should always carry out a small test on the surface intended for decoration. Either choose a spot that is out of sight, such as on a wall at the back of a cupboard, or one that is not a focal point, such as near the skirting board.

SPONGING

Dab sponge gently over the design, taking care not to fill the area with too much paint.

DRAGGING WITH A BRUSH

Simply drag the brush over the design, working in one direction only.

STIPPLING

For the original stencilling method, hold the brush upright and use a dabbing motion.

SHADING WITH TWO COLOURS

Stencil on the first colour. When dry, take a darker colour and work from centre to edge.

EDGING

With a circular motion, work the brush around the edge, leaving the centre white.

Paper or card

Most paints (poster, oil, gouache etc) and fibre tip pens can be used on paper and card, but for the best results you should use fabric paint or artists' acrylic, as it gives a smoother finish than most, and is permanent. You can buy stencil stationery kits which include stencils, brushes, suitable paints, cards and envelopes.

Plaster

Many different effects can be achieved by stencilling directly onto bare plaster, using different media (see page 116). First prime the walls with a clear universal sealant to reduce the porosity of the plaster. Allow 24 hours for this to dry.

Note: *For all methods, secure the stencil using low-tack masking tape or spray adhesive. Whether using a brush or sponge, always dab off excess paint on absorbent paper before you start.*

Note: *For a solid colour, work the paint well into the design to establish a thick coat. Take care not to overload the brush, or the paint will run under the stencil and smudge. Alternatively, if you want a soft colour, a very faint look can be achieved by using an almost dry brush and gently stencilling with a circular motion, working from the outside to the centre.*

Note: *If you find that you have stencilled your project too strongly, it is easy to soften the colour. Simply replace the stencil over the design, taking care to line it up properly. With a little white paint, gently brush over the design.*

CREATING A TILED LOOK

1 Divide the area into a grid and draw with a pencil. Cheat a little if necessary to make sure the squares fit.

Note: *It is always a good idea to make up bedcovers and curtains before stencilling, to ensure that the pattern falls properly.*

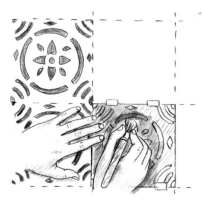

2 Cut the tile design and work out a pattern on paper before you start. Attach stencil with masking tape and stencil within the grid.

3 Draw in grout lines with permanent fibre tip pen or cut a line out of stencil material.

Fabric

Always wash any new fabric to remove traces of size. You can stencil on most fabrics, but the success of the colour will depend on the fibre content and the finish of the cloth. Natural fibres respond best, because they absorb the dyes well, but mixes like polyester/cotton are also successful. Glazed fabrics, like chintzes, are more difficult to work with, because the paint sits on top of the surface.

Ceramics

You should use ceramic paint. However, nothing is permanent on a glazed ceramic surface unless fired (see page 121) so, after decorating, seal it with ceramic sealant or polyurethane.

To stencil on gloss ceramic tiles, coat them with undercoat or eggshell finish paint first, then stencil with acrylics, and finally seal with polyurethane.

Metal

Metal should be prepared for decoration by removing any rust with a wire brush, rubbing down with steel wool, and finally priming with a metal primer. Either stencil with sprays, or use enamel paint applied with the dry brush method.

Wood

If you wish to stencil on natural wood, it is essential to remove any dirt, polish, wax, lacquer and varnish. Dirt and polish can be taken off with a solution of equal quantities of white (mineral) spirit and raw linseed oil, plus a dash of vinegar. Use a soft cloth, or fine grade steel wool if the old finish proves particularly stubborn.

If the main finish under this is wax or oil, you will be able to cut it back with white (mineral) spirit to reach the bare wood. However, if the spirit fails to penetrate to the wood, this means the finish is either shellac-based, or a cellulose-type lacquer or varnish. Shellac and most old varnishes can be removed with methylated spirits (denatured alcohol), though you should be careful when working on veneered pieces, as meths can lift the glue that holds the veneer in position. Cellulose-based varnish and lacquer can be dissolved using liquid paint stripper, or a commercial product which is designed specifically for fine furniture, as it does not raise the grain of the wood. To remove a paint finish use a liquid paint stripper, or have the piece dipped in caustic soda (lye).

Finally, if in removing the finish the grain of the wood has been raised, it must be sanded down, beginning with a coarse grade of paper and progressing to a finer grade. And any knots that have been exposed should be treated with a knotting compound, to prevent resin from blistering or staining the stencilling.

You will find that timber dyes produce interesting effects on wood. As they are of a very thin consistency they should be applied with a very dry brush. Add a spot of varnish to thicken them slightly.

Bleached-look wood

If you wish to stencil on a limed wood, you should remove any paint, wax or varnish with a liquid paint stripper, and then scour the surface with coarse steel wool and a wire brush – always in the direction of the grain. This will open up the grain, and allow you to create a bleached look by rubbing white emulsion paint, tinted with a spot of grey acrylic, into the surface.

Painted surfaces

A painted surface that is badly chipped or peeling will need treatment to prevent the stencilling flaking off soon after it is applied. Either you will have to strip off the old finish with liquid stripper or a blowtorch, and then repaint it, or rub it down, using progressively fine grades of sandpaper, until you have achieved a smooth surface that can be recoated.

However, a sound, painted surface does not necessarily provide a suitable base for stencilling. A gloss finish will need rubbing back, or keying, so that the stencil paints will adhere to it. In fact, it is better to give

it an eggshell finish, stencil, and then re-apply the sheen by coating with a silk finish varnish on top.

Finally, if you have had to recoat a surface with paint prior to stencilling, always allow plenty of time for it to dry. Even water-based paints, which seem to dry so quickly, can still release moisture if they are covered too soon. This can blister or lift off the stencilling later on.

Plastic laminates and melamine

First wash down the surface and leave overnight to dry. Wipe over again using methylated spirits (denatured alcohol) on a cotton rag. Then rub down using wet and dry abrasive paper wet with plenty of soap to act as a lubricant. Apply one coat of eggshell paint. Finally, stencil on top using any stencil paint. This treatment must be confined to furniture; any surface that comes into contact with food, such as a worktop or plate, should never be painted. To decorate melamine plates with stencilling, a special method can be used (see page 104).

Ceramic tiles

With tiles that are already laid, remove most of the existing grout. Make sure that the surface is clean and dry. There is no need for an undercoat – just paint directly with an eggshell finish. Leave for a week until it is hard, then regrout. Stencil with acrylic paints. With new tiles, buy the satin finish type, then use ceramic paints and seal (see above), or use on-glaze enamel applied heavily and then fired in (see page 121).

Vitreous enamel

When painting directly on the outside of baths and basins, most stencillers coat with paint then stencil with acrylics. It is important to use an oil-based paint, such as eggshell, on cast iron baths in order to prevent possible leaching of rust from the metal beneath. The interior presents a greater problem, and therefore you need advice from paint experts.

Note: *When using paint strippers, follow any instructions on the tin or bottle very carefully.*

COPING WITH CORNERS

VARIATIONS ON ONE BORDER

The basic stencil border.

*Bells and leaf shapes used to make a
straight line border.*

*The simple bell shape is used upright and
inverted to make a deep border.*

*Leaf shapes arranged in a t-shape to make
a geometric design.*

*Let the border flow around the
corner, leaving out some parts
of the design and filling in
shapes in other parts.*

*Leaf and bell shapes arranged to form a tile
motif. A ruler is used to draw the 'tile'
outline.*

*To mitre the corner, draw a
diagonal line and place masking
tape to one side of this line.
Stencil up to the tape. Remove
tape and repeat the other side of
the design. Place the border at
right angles to the next one.
Stencil a single corner motif and
space the border stencils to meet
them.*

Concrete
Make sure that the concrete is thoroughly
dry. Sprinkle water on the surrounding
area to minimise the possibility of dust
rising and sticking to the paint. Use chlorinated rubber paints for maximum life
underfoot.

Glass
Stencilling on glass can take on the look of
etched or stained glass. Use either auto
spray paints or special glass paints (see
page 21).

FLOORS

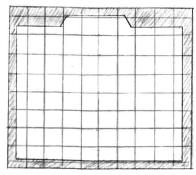

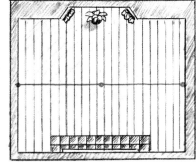

1 *Measure the floor.*

2 *Mark the centre of each opposite skirting board, join with a straight chalk line across the room and mark the centre.*

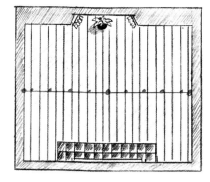

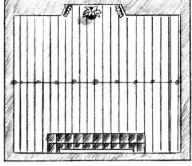

3 *Starting at this central point, mark off points corresponding to the stencil widths at intervals along this line.*

4 *At the edge of the stencil that falls nearest each wall, draw a line at right angles to the centre line.*

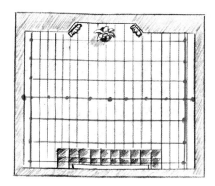

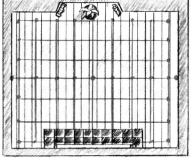

5 *Mark off the stencil widths along these two lines and join.*

6 *Complete the grid by joining the points.*

VARNISHING YOUR DESIGN

It is not essential to varnish stencilling on walls, but for a large area, such as a stencilled mural, a protective coating will save it from damage. Spray varnishes are the easiest to use. If using polyurethane, thin down the first coat for easier application (three parts varnish to one part white/mineral spirit).

For furniture, floors or any situation where water resistance is needed, polyurethane is essential for a durable finish. The disadvantage of polyurethane is that it does tend to yellow. Brands vary – the palest are preferable, but you will only find out which you like best with experience. On the whole, the 'professional' type are slightly better. The yellowing is more prominent over tints of blue. Interestingly, experts counteract the yellowing by adding a touch of cobalt blue artists' oil colour. The number of coats you use will also affect yellowing, so avoid more than one coat on areas like tiles, where resistance to water and grease is the only requirement. Floors, of course, will require several layers.

Gloss polyurethane is harder wearing than satin or matte, but if a duller finish is preferred, apply two coats of gloss, then finish with a satin coat. Five coats, each well-thinned, will give as hard-wearing a result as three coats unthinned and will also minimise discoloration.

BACKGROUND TECHNIQUES

DRAGGING

SPONGING

RAG ROLLING

PAINT TECHNIQUES AS BACKGROUNDS TO STENCILS

There are various ways of creating paint effects, but all of them require one colour as a base coat, and at least one other as a top coat.

Dragging

A dragged surface gives the appearance of a streaky fabric, wood grain or raw silk. Paint a base coat, using an eggshell or silk water-based paint, and let it dry. Now prepare a glaze. Professional decorators use a ready-made transparent glaze, known as scumble or flatting oil. To this they add an equal quantity of white (mineral) spirit, and then tint it with a colour, using either gloss paint or artists' oils. An alternative method of making a glaze is to add an equal quantity of water to coloured silk paint. Unfortunately this does not stay wet for as long as scumble, so you will need to work more rapidly.

Apply the glaze sparingly to the surface to be decorated. Then take a dry brush and, holding it almost flat against the surface, brush firmly but lightly, either from top to bottom or from side to side, in one continuous sweep. Keep a constant pressure, reducing it only slightly at the end of each sweep, to avoid a build-up of colour. Wipe the dragging brush every few strokes – if it becomes loaded with glaze it will put colour on, rather than take it off. When the glaze is dry you can stencil, and then varnish with matte or eggshell finish polyurethane to protect it.

Sponging

Sponging has a softer appearance than dragging, giving a blotted ink or cloudy effect. First paint on a base coat of eggshell or matte, and let it dry. The base coat should always be lighter than any of the sponged coats that follow. You now have a choice. Either you can sponge off, or you can sponge on.

To sponge off, brush on a glaze, and

then dab a natural sponge over it, abruptly but evenly, to lift off some of the colour. Every so often clean the sponge, either in water or white (mineral) spirit – depending on whether the glaze is spirit- or water-based.

To sponge on, spread glaze or emulsion (latex) on a plate, and use the natural sponge to dab it on top of the base coat. Take care not to overload the sponge or you will end up with thick, wet prints. Keep dabbing until a cloudy effect develops. Let it dry, then stencil, and finally coat with silk or matte polyurethane.

Rag rolling

This technique gives a random effect that looks like lightly crumpled fabric. Paint on a base coat and prepare a glaze in the same way as for dragging and sponging. Next choose a rag: experiment with various fabrics such as cotton, velvet and chamois leather. They will all give a slightly different effect. However, avoid dyed fabrics, as the colour can rub off, and only use lint-free materials. Again, you have a choice of ragging on or off.

To rag off, brush the glaze over the surface. Take your rag and soak it in white (mineral) spirit or water, depending on the base of the glaze. Roll it over the surface of the glaze, as if rolling pastry in all directions. Work at various angles, avoiding the vertical and horizontal. Keep changing the position of the rag, and keep cleaning or swopping it to avoid a build-up of colour – you are taking it off, not putting it on.

To rag on, simply follow the same technique, except this time you will be dipping the rag in the glaze from time to time as you put it on.

ALL-OVER DESIGNS ON WALLS AND FLOORS

All-over designs are among the most tricky to tackle, and require a great deal of thought and planning before starting.

First, you must measure the size of the area that you intend to decorate, and then draw a scale plan on paper, in order to establish how many repeats will be required. It is possible that you will need to adjust the plan slightly at this stage, so that the overall pattern is balanced. For example, you may find that there is a focal point in the room around which the design needs to be centred, such as an interlinking doorway or a fireplace. It is important to stencil a complete pattern around these important features, whereas on or around less significant areas, such as skirtings, window surrounds and corners hidden by furniture, you can get away with half a motif.

To transfer the pattern from paper to the wall or floor, you should mark out the surface into a grid, using a hard pencil or chalk, a ruler and a set-square, and copy the design square by square.

CORRECTING MISTAKES

How you deal with mistakes will depend on your attitude. Many experts will work mistakes into designs, or 'cheat', so that the error is less evident. There are no rules to stencilling. If the stencil doesn't quite fit the space, you can always add half of the design . . . a flower bud, a few leaves etc. However, you should be prepared for slips by keeping a damp cloth to hand, and by reserving some background paint to cover up any disasters.

If, when you've completed the stencilling and the paint is dry, you stand back and you aren't happy with the result, you can remove most of it by rubbing with a scouring pad and either some warm water and detergent, or white (mineral) spirit. Then re-establish the base coat with a single coat of paint, allowing you to start again.

Note: *With paint effects, always work from light to dark when you build up layers of colour. If you find that some areas are becoming too dark, just wipe them down and start again.*

Note: *It's a good idea to mark the centre of the wall or floor too. Do this by stretching a length of string from one corner to the one diagonally opposite, repeat with the remaining corners and mark the point where the two lengths meet.*

INDEX

Page numbers in *italics* refer to information in captions.

BIBLIOGRAPHY/FURTHER READING

The Art of Decorative Stencilling, Adele Bishop and Cile Lord. Penguin

Early American Stencils on Walls and Furniture, Janet Waring, New York

Flower Painting, Jenny Rodwell, Macdonald

Interior Affairs, Alex Davidson, Ward Lock

Lyn Le Grice's Art of Stencilling, Viking

Ornament, Stuart Durant, Macdonald

Paint Magic Jocasta Innes

Paris Graffiti, Joerg Huber, Thames and Hudson

Putting back the Style, Ed Alexandra Artley, Evans

Surfaces and Finishes, Penny Radford, Macmillan

Techniques in American Folk Decoration, Jean Lipman, Eve Meulendyke; Dover

The Decorated Tile, J and B Austwick, Pitman House

The Grammar of Ornament, Owen Jones, Studio Editions

The Modern Painter and Decorator, Arthur Seymour Jennings and Guy Cadogan Rothery, Caxton.

Acknowledgements

The authors would like to thank the following for opening their doors to us: Jane and Malcolm Jackson; Carol Grainger; Jackie and Paul Khara; Mrs Andrews, Ann Lizzimore; Carol and Mark Crompton; Louise and Terry Redhead; Sarah and Richard Bethell; Anne Elkington; Ian and Francesca Murray; Vanessa and Larry De Waay; Mr and Mrs Howes; Esther and Brian Howlett; Kit and Bob Deal; Ann and Nick Simons; Anne Mackenzie and Harry.
Also thanks to Wards Nurseries of Sarratt (especially Mr Rawlings and John); the staff at Watford branches of Habitat, The Reject Shop and Perrings; Scoops of Amersham; Elizabeth Macleod Matthews of Chenies Manor; Pat Fallan; David and Gill of David Smith Interiors.
For their technical and historic advice: Mr Gibbs of Campbell Smith and Company; Mr Cook of Technical Paint Services; Tom Pearson of Crown Paints.
And for their help on the projects: Essential transporting: Steve Brightwell; Marbling: Fred Wieland and Pam Lennon; Stencilling fabric: Julia Boyce; Ceramics: Marion Calvert; Speedy curtain making: Jennie Emery, Jean Gregory; Peter Emery for late night DIY and special thanks to Saleena Khara for both her stencilling and immaculate needlework.
And not least thanks to Marion and Alan for prompt special deliveries and a first class sitting service.

STENCIL MANUFACTURERS

Laura Ashley. Branches worldwide. Mail order details from PO Box 19, Newton, Powys, Wales, SY16 4LG.
Adele Bishop, PO Box 3349, Kinston, NC 28501. Distributed in UK by Carolyn Warrender Designs.
Felicity Binyon and Elizabeth Macfarlane, 6 Polstead Road, Oxford, OX2 6TN.
Lyn le Grice Stencil Design Ltd, Bread Street, Penzance, Cornwall, TR18 2EQ.
Pavilion, 6A Howe Street, Edinburgh, EH3 6TD.
Paintability, 9 Heneage Street, London, E1 5LJ.
Stencil Decor, Eurostudio, Plaid Enterprises, Box 7600, Norcross, GA 30091; UK: Eurostudio Ltd, Unit 4 Southdown Industrial Estate, Southdown Road, Harpenden, Herts, AL5 1PW.
Stencil Ease, New Ipswich, NH 03071. Distributed in UK by Carolyn Warrender Deigns.
Stencil-itis, PO Box 30, Rickmansworth, Herts, WD3 5LG.
Carolyn Warrender Designs, PO Box 358, London, SW11 4NR.
Many of these companies also sell stencilling products such as paints, crayons, Mylar, card and brushes.

STENCILLERS

Unless otherwise stated, all the special projects in this book were stencilled by Michael Flinn.
Other stencillers were:
Ruth Barclay, 22 Loudoun Road, London, NW8 0LT; Robert and Colleen Bery, 8 Rosehill Road, London, SW18 2NX; Felicity Binyon/Elizabeth Macfarlane, address above; Ann Chiswell Designs, 34 Queen's Drive, London, W3 0HA; Gaby McCall, Little Orchards, Balcombe, Nr Haywards Heath, Sussex; Julia Roberts, The Farm, The Green, Letchmore Heath, Herts, WD2 8ES; Verona Stencilling, Gorhambury, St Albans, Herts; Melanie Stock, Chantry Farmhouse, Beaminster, Dorset; Paul Treadaway, 31 Elm Tree Green, Great Missenden, Bucks; Fred Wieland, PO Box 30, Rickmansworth, Herts.

MANUFACTURERS AND DISTRIBUTORS

Pebeo St-Marcel, 13367, Marseille Cedex 11. Distributed in UK by A. West and Partners Products Ltd, 684 Mitcham Road, Croydon, CR9 3AB. Acrylics, ceramic, glass and fabric paints.
Dylon International Ltd, Worsley Bridge Road, Lower Sydenham, London, SE26 5HD. Fabric paint and fabric felt pens.
Duncan Ceramic Products, Fresno, California 93727. Distributed in UK by Claygaze Ltd, Talbot Road, Rickmansworth, Herts. Bisq stain (universal paint) and ceramic sealer.
Technical Paint Services, Horton Bridge Road, West Drayton, Middlesex.
Chlorinated rubber paint; general paints
Bell China Paints, USA. Distributed in UK by Claygaze (as above). On-glaze.
The Ceramic Craft and Colour Company, Unit 8, Whitebridge Lane, Stone, Staffordshire, ST15 8LQ. Craft Colours for use on wood, plaster, ceramic and porcelain bisque, glass, plastics, pre primed metals and fabrics.
Sterling Roncraft, Chapeltown, Sheffield, S30 4YP. Translac professional polyurethane varnish.
J W Bollom and Co, 314 Old Brompton Road, London, SW5. Vinyl wall glaze.
Maecher Pictureproducts Ltd, PO Box 9, Snodland, Kent, ME6 5LW. Maecher Melamine Pictureproducts, PO Box 112, North Richmond 2754, New South Wales, Australia. Melamine plates.

The authors would like to thank the following manufacturers for supplying materials for photography: Ametex Fabrics (UK), G.P. & J. Baker, W.M. Christy & Sons, Dorma, Philip Edwards Ltd, Forbo Nairn, Anna French Ltd, Harrison Drape, Hunter Douglas, H. & R. Johnson, Laura Ashley, Limericks Linens, Osborne & Little, Arthur Sanderson & Sons Ltd, Crown Paints, Dulux Paints, Holts Lloyd Ltd, A. West & Partners, Addis, And So to Bed, BHS, Czech & Speake, Maecher Picture Products, Stevenson Brothers, Trellisworks, Villeroy & Boch, Felicity Binyon and Elizabeth Macfarlane, Lyn le Grice Stencil Design Ltd, Pavilion, Pebeo, Stencil Decor, Stencil Ease, Stencil-itis, Carolyn Warrender Designs, Rain.